# VOLUNTEERISM
## AND
# WORLD DEVELOPMENT

# VOLUNTEERISM AND WORLD DEVELOPMENT

## Pathway to a New World

## Allen Jedlicka

New York
Westport, Connecticut
London

**Library of Congress Cataloging-in-Publication Data**

Jedlicka, Allen D.
    Volunteerism and world development : pathway to a new world /
Allen Jedlicka.
        p.    cm.
    Includes bibliographical references.
    ISBN 0-275-93241-9 (alk. paper)
    1. Volunteerism.    2. Economic development.    I. Title.
HN49.V64J43    1990
361.3'7—dc20            89-49173

Library of Congress Catalog Card Number: 89-49173
ISBN: 0-275-93241-9

First published in 1990

Praeger Publishers, One Madison Avenue, New York, NY 10010
An imprint of Greenwood Publishing Group, Inc.

Printed in the United States of America

∞

The paper used in this book complies with the
Permanent Paper Standard issued by the National
Information Standards Organization (Z39.48-1984).

10 9 8 7 6 5 4 3 2 1

# Contents

# Preface

Through much of our history as a democratic nation, we have had problems with the constructive administration of government-controlled bureaucracies. The sad truth is that too often, government-controlled bureaucracies have not justly served the people they are responsible too. For example, in the 1970s the Social Security Administration was accused of improperly eliminating benefits to certain classes of handicapped people. In the 1980s the disclosures of how HUD money was allowed to be squandered by bureaucrats and real estate developers at the expense of poor people disgusted the average citizen. And in the 1990s and 2000s, given this past history, there will probably be similar abuses.

But these historical cases and projections of abuses to come shouldn't be surprising, for while such behavior is appalling, it occurs from mechanistic and organizational processes that are inevitable in large bureaucracies. The simple fact is that bureaucracies are not effective vehicles to address the social and economic concerns of people. The primary behavior of a bureaucracy is organizational survival and rewards to those who run the bureaucracy—not that service to a target group of people be maximized. That reality has important implications for development efforts in the Third World: Quite simply, big bureaucracies can't do it.

What happened to HUD in the 1980s—its failure to work for the people to whom it is responsible—has happened over and over in bureaucratic efforts to help Third World people and will happen over and over again if we continue to rely on such an inherently inept, institutional means of carrying out change.

In my experience there has always been a distinct difference between bureaucratic and volunteer service in world-development efforts. The key difference is that volunteer efforts, free of the corrupt influences that affect bureaucracies, are more often successful in directly helping clients—because there is no motive to abuse the people they serve.

This is to say that the volunteer's motives to help are purer because, by definition, the environmental factors that affect the bureaucratic process—greed, institutional survival, and a basic indifference to people—do not enter the picture. People volunteer and work for nothing because they want to help other people, not because they want to control or direct others, or collect six-figure consulting fees.

Thus, if we are to speak of a real world development, the institutional factors that impede that process must be removed. And that means, to the furthest extent possible, we must eliminate the involvement of bureaucracies and substitute a more direct, person-to-person process. Volunteers are most amenable to that process, and the purpose of this book is to show how volunteers—even on a macro level—are more effective in helping people than bureaucracies can be. Accordingly, Chapter 2 will show why bureaucracies are essentially worthless in creating a true world development; and Chapters 3, 4, and 5 will discuss why—on the other hand—volunteers are more appropriate in accomplishing that objective.

But if we are going to rely on volunteer means to carry out a world development, there must be a change in the minds and values of the average citizen. And what will be the means of changing those values? The readers will perhaps be not surprised to find that I suggest the educational system. But they may be surprised by my suggestion that operant conditioning (or as some people would say, brainwashing)—combined with community and parent involvement—would be the most rapid and effective means of changing popular values. The writings and work of B. F. Skinner are especially relevant in this context.

We already know that, for the majority of American children in the 1980s, the family has failed in providing any baseline sense of values. This has come about partly as a result of changing economic conditions. Two-earner families (and most are two earner by necessity—not choice) do not have much time to spend with their children. So too, many of our children get their values from violent television programs and drug-using peers before Mama and Daddy come home from work, and too many parents provide inadequate role models by abusing drugs themselves.

Who spends the most time with the kids? It is the schools: from 8:00 A.M. to 3:30 P.M. And that influence and involvement will probably become even larger. For example, several pilot programs that place preschoolers into day-care centers at local schools have been so successful that there is serious talk of implementing such programs throughout the country. This could mean that soon the major influence on our children from ages 1–18 will be their schools. With so dramatic an influence lies the possibility of training people to be concerned about their relationship to other people and other cultures, to become citizens who support volunteer efforts that help other people and create a new world. This can be done through the educational system, provided we make institutional changes that will complement the internalization of such values in our children.

Two classic pedagogical techniques that come into play in this educational process involve the providing of information and critical skills along with it—so as to be able to assess the information one is given—and the teaching of organizational skills such as how to mobilize small groups. But we must add to this the use of operant conditioning, or the reinforcement of values supportive of changing the human condition and creating a true global community. The ultimate objective is to create citizens who, after receiving an education that emphasizes global concerns, will be motivated to play a volunteer role in creating an equitable world for all people. To produce values that will effect such an internalized motivation, we must use behavioral technologies that can rapidly generate a conducive state of being.

This is where operant conditioning (still highly controversial even forty years after B. F. Skinner's *Walden II*) comes in. Its implementation will be presented in Chapter 7.

The predominant theme of this book, therefore, is that volunteer efforts will be more effective in creating a new world than will bureaucratic efforts. But there is still a function for government in all this: It can provide the funding and the legislation that will help and encourage volunteers to do the job, while yet keeping state bureaucracies out of the process to the maximum degree possible. As such, in this kind of democracy, congressmen would become facilitators to volunteer groups and would provide the logistical and monetary support to the volunteers actually doing the job.

In spite of the social-program miserliness of the United States at this point in history, some of this is already happening. One good example is the 1980 New York State Good Samaritan Act, which allows restaurants to give leftover prepared food to volunteer agencies that feed the homeless (with the restaurants protected from lawsuit, should someone get sick from the food). The same law allows donated out-of-code and prepared foods to be claimed as tax deductions by the restaurants and grocery stores cooperating with volunteer agencies. That sure beats throwing it away; and all the parties involved have gained something, as well. Chapters 5 and 6 cite examples of how government can become even more creative—providing equipment and logistical support to volunteers in what amounts to governmental overload expenses, without creating another worthless Washington bureaucracy to mismanage the program. This is not mere academic hypothesizing. Legislative measures such as the Good Samaritan Act show that we can do this if we really want to.

But to effectively develop volunteerism, an element of organization must accompany the process from the start, as well as a management style compatible to the needs of people when they are working without pay. Chapters 4 and 5 discuss the need for a participative management foundation and show how equal responsibilities in control and decision making can be provided to all the members of a voluntary organization. Autocratic management approaches have little applicability to healthy organizations of any kind in the late twentieth century, and absolutely none in a volunteer organization. Unfortunately, I must necessarily limit my discussion of management processes in this book. But the reader may supplement his or her understanding by reading two other books of mine published with Praeger. The first, *Organization for Rural Development* (1977), discusses the elements of participative management, small group development, and extensive service as they relate to Third World development. The second, *Organizational Change and the Third World* (1987), shows how organizational development and change techniques can be utilized by Third World bureaucracies to serve more effectively the people of their countries.

In a sense, this third book closes the series. The ultimate step is not only to develop the Third World, but to create a whole new world in which all people become dedicated to helping each other, to sharing the world's wealth, and to eliminating the bureaucratic and political processes that have wasted so much of the Earth's resources. I have tried to explain how we can begin that process, in this book.

I think we have reached the point in human evolution where this kind of talk is not meaningless. The crisis circumstances of environmental degradation and population increases force us to conceive of creative solutions to the problems we face. And this will have to be done on a personal basis, for large bureaucratic institutions have long since proven that they do not work.

If we are to find these creative solutions and chart our way to a new world, the development of volunteerism must be considered a serious and most viable path of action. I hope I'll have convinced you of that route by the end of this book.

# VOLUNTEERISM
## AND
# WORLD DEVELOPMENT

# ONE

# A New World:
# With a Little Bit of Luck,
# We Can Make It?

The twenty-first century is almost upon us, and the primary task of the early decades of that new millennium will be to develop the organizational (and possibly even the spiritual) means of sharing the economic resources of the planet with all of its human citizens. However, while humans will live very differently as time goes on, human nature is likely to remain—as it has since the caveman—undeveloped and unevolving. While the human ability to solve problems has improved, mankind's humanity has not.

Those preoccupied with the future think that small wars are more likely than big wars in the next century. Terrorists from the countless ranks of the have-nots will be more apt to create world tension then will the major powers, and hunger is more likely than ideology to bring about war. But we all know there will be changes, for by the year 2100 the population of the world is expected to double from 4.9 billion to 10.4 billion. The poorest nations—in Africa, Asia, and Latin America—will have the most people, and the richest may have a hard time enjoying their dinner. Market regions will necessarily shift as the developed countries drop from a quarter to a seventh of the world population. "Economically, the center of Western Civilization will shift from the U.S. and Europe to the U.S. and the Pacific. U.S. trade with Asia will double that with Europe for stripped of empire, Europe's share of world commerce has already shrunk to a fraction of what it was in 1900."[1] This is just one of the many futurist scenarios being proposed as we approach the year 2000. But of particular interest to the central message of this book is the aforementioned prediction that world hunger is more likely to bring war than ideology ever did. Certainly we have here a motivating factor behind world development; and indeed, as the Western and Soviet Pact countries pursue their talks, ideology does seem to be going out the window and the impact of hunger receiving more attention. One can only hope that such dialogue will continue. The international conflict we may face in finally getting a grip on the establishment of an equitable world development can greatly exceed—and may reduce to child's play—the ideological battles we have faced during the past forty years.

For at the base of resolving the global hunger and development problem is the fact that, to create an equitable global system and to develop a new world, there must be a major change in the way citizens of the developed countries view the rest of the world, as well as a new international order (not the international order being demanded now by the Group of 77, but one that is workable and acceptable to all countries).

And underlying all of this is the simple irony that human nature (that is, the "civilized" nature established 10,000 years ago) no longer serves us. Fortunately, as this book hopes to show, human nature can be changed—which is not to suggest that it will be easy. This changed human nature can play an effective volunteer role in creating a new world, and will stand in stark contrast to the development efforts carried out by traditional development organizations working in the various nation-states. Based on their dismal record over the past thirty years, one may predict that such organizations will do no better in the next century. There are too many institutional barriers that prevent them from doing an effective, people-oriented job (see Chapter 2). Changing those organizations to the degree that they become creative, participative organisms capable of doing the job right is equally unlikely. Research and experience show that past efforts along these lines have not been good.[2]

If such organizations as the United Nations were to dissolve their existing development agencies—so as to foster new agencies with a more participative, needs-oriented philosophical base—it might be ultimately possible to produce a developmental infrastructure that would be more effective in helping people. But given the thousands of worthless professional bureaucrats and technicians (many with relatives or dirty pictures helping them to maintain their current positions) who would be terminated by such a move, the possibility of it happening is probably less than zero. There is just too much vested interest in what exists to lead one to believe that it will ever really reform itself.

Given this pessimistic scenario of institutional change, one must look to other means of affecting a world development (one sustained by the financial resources of the existing network of nations that provide international development aid). The means that I prefer is development of a global volunteer effort that will remain free of the limitations and political constraints hampering the professional change model. Proposing volunteerism as a viable means of creating a world development is the purpose of this book.

Various rationales behind the use of a volunteer means of development will be described in subsequent chapters. However, what all these rationales share in common is a belief that the helping of others must come purely from a sense of humanitarian obligation.

The problem with Western world-development efforts in the past (with their vague Christian linkages basing them somewhat on a sense of philanthropy and concern for global neighbors) is that most development efforts are sponsored by nation-states and are more often than not based on a compromised philanthropy—a philanthropy that expects a direct gain for the donor.

Consequently, when the United States provided extensive aid to Honduras in the 1980s for agriculture and rural education (especially with increasing evidence that the generals of that country were engaged in drug running), one would not have to be very cynical to suspect that the aid had something to do with

4    Volunteerism and World Development

the U.S. National Guard training camps and the Contra "youth hostels" that were suddenly cropping up on the Honduran landscape.

## VOLUNTEERISM AND PERSONAL HEALTH

One way of eliminating such compromised philanthropy is to eliminate the pecuniary and political rewards to the players. Were we to send 2,000 Iowa farmers to Honduras for the summer, paying only their round-trip transport (which would cost about $1 million), we'd do no worse—and probably better—than what we get for that $150 million running a professional agriculture-development program. Given that professionals exhibit severe limitations when it comes to helping people, then volunteers can be seen as a key element in our world-development proposition. By definition, volunteerism eliminates the corrupt end-products of professional, nation-sponsored development efforts: It includes no expectation of reciprocity.

Nevertheless, there are advantages both to the recipients of volunteer help and to the volunteers themselves. Recent research has shown that volunteerism benefits the physical and mental health of the volunteer. One researcher in the field, Allan Luks of the Institute for Advancement of Health, argues convincingly that there occurs among members of a volunteer work group the release of endorphins (certain body chemicals) that promote a sense of well-being and contribute significantly to extending the individual's life expectancy.[3] The prescribed dosage for this benefit is five hours of volunteer work a week. More recent research also shows that even thinking about and planning volunteer efforts can provide similar health benefits, but not so extensively.

What is particularly interesting about the latter finding is that it substantiates some of the basic tenets of Christianity (those that so often in its history have not been practiced): the Golden Rule, and the conviction that helping those who are not so fortunate will also help one's self.

What is also particularly interesting is that the direct participation of the individual produces the life-extension chemicals.

Giving money to a philanthropic organization just won't have the same effect (although it may make you feel good). You actually have to mix it up with other volunteer members and with the people being helped. You have to participate in the process.

If this health-benefit phenomenon can be verified to be true, then it will be a fortunate promotional tool in creating a volunteer-based world development. For one thing, in the first stages of organizing the process, a major source of volunteer labor will be from retired or semiretired people. (Later, as we change the educational system, younger and younger people will become integrated into the process—which is the subject of Chapter 7). The majority of those early world-development pioneers, therefore, will be people to whom a few more good years would not be unwelcome. Is it possible that doctors will end up prescribing volunteerism as a routine therapy for the middle aged?

What is most amazing is the obviousness of all this. How many times have we told ourselves how good it feels to help other people? How many times have we returned home after such an experience with the glow of goodwill upon us? This may all sound very unscientific, and yet science is beginning to confirm these same folk feelings as having a real basis in human physiology.

Unfortunately, many present-day Americans are far removed from this sort of direct involvement in the caring for others. This doesn't mean that they can't change. And if one may believe in societal cycles, U.S. society could be headed for a more caring cycle, similar to that of the 1960s. So why not promote the generous side of the human condition. It certainly can't hurt volunteer programs any, and may entice certain people to join this or that volunteer effort when they otherwise wouldn't.

## THE COUNTERPART TO PROFESSIONALISM

Viewed from the perspective of an altruistic and personal-health paradigm, the problem with professional organizations may be that the institutional environment represses the ability of the individual to behave in a humanistic way toward the people that the organization is supposed to be serving. Orga-

nizational process and institution building replaces a concern
for the ultimate objective of significantly helping a particular
population of people. (This will be discussed in greater detail in
Chapter 2). Is it possible that becoming an "organization man"
can really make a person give up his or her underlying humanness? Or does that person get psychologically trapped and wind
up trading humanness for a position in the organization?

Still another recent finding—a genetic reality—may affirm the
basic human need to help others that professional bureaucrats
seem so effectively to ignore. Present in every human being's
mitochondria DNA is the historical reality that all humans came
from one protomodern woman in Africa about 200,000 years
ago. That is to say, science is now telling us that indeed we are
all brothers and sisters.[4] Could it be that this ancestral com-
monality in our genes compels us to be inherently concerned
about others and programmed to help them—which then produces a physiological balance that promotes longevity? That's
not inconceivable: Science continues to explain away the bound-
aries between mind and matter. And it is especially applicable
to volunteers, who work not for money but for the good of their
brothers and sisters.

Consequently, for the reasons just mentioned and more, this
book holds that volunteerism—based on an underlying need to
engage in altruistic behavior toward fellow human beings—is a
mechanism that will complement a world development. It is only
natural that we should feel compelled to help our brothers and
sisters. Volunteerism is an organized way we can do that without
compromising our inherently programmed philanthropy.

## VOLUNTEERISM AND COMMUNICATIONS
## TECHNOLOGY

To complement the inherent desire for volunteerism, there
must be available a technology that maximizes efficiency in
working on world-development projects. Volunteers will depend increasingly on a reasonably priced means of communication that can enable them to implement effective and
inexpensive solutions to global problems. (This will be discussed
thoroughly in Chapter 6.)

Fortunately, the communications revolution has arrived, for the electronic tools of today and tomorrow complement the higher-order, altruistic function of humans and eliminate the time-consuming drudgery of so much that had to be done by hand in earlier times. B. F. Skinner is quite correct when he comments that

as technology advances machines will take over more and more of the functions of men, but only up to a point. We build machines which reduce some of the aversive features of our environment (grueling labor, for example) and which produce more positive reinforcers. We build them precisely because they do so. . . . If the machines man makes eventually make him wholly expendable, it will be by accident, not design.[5]

For the global development effort I am proposing, machines will in no way make the human being expendable. On the contrary, in the case of cross-national development teams, advanced communication instruments will certainly expand, amplify, and complement a development consulting group's ability to work with counterparts in the countries they serve.

The consultants could even operate out of their living rooms, if they so choose—thanks to the miniaturization of computer technology over the past forty years. Telephone modems allow connections to be made via new low-cost communication satellites, accessing the entire world with a home transmitting device the size of a small suitcase. And coming on-line by the mid–1990s will be low-cost instant (human voice–simulated) translators that allow participants without foreign language capability to communicate internationally, regardless.

In short, we have reached the point in technological evolution where global communication is no longer the property of large corporations and governments, but the domain of all people. Even as recently as ten years ago we could not have spoken seriously of an integrated volunteer world-development effort because the communication technology was not cheap enough to fit the budgets of volunteer programs.

There are many low-cost technological systems that have come from the communications revolution, and they will be presented for discussion in Chapter 6. But key to the implementation of

any global volunteerism is its access through democratic managerial systems and governments. Without a supporting framework of democracy, volunteer development activities and
technology are fighting an uphill battle. The link between democracy and volunteerism will therefore be studied in the following section.

## DEMOCRACY AND VOLUNTEERISM

The United States has always claimed a special place in the
world because it was the first to establish itself as a democratic
government, which in its simplest form means that the people
rule. Throughout our 200 years of history, we as a nation seem
to have felt destined to lead the rest of humanity to truth and
justice, and to promote the American Way of Life as the prototype for a better world.

It's not surprising that we haven't always been able to live up
to such high expectations, for from the start there were flaws in
our system of democracy (slavery and an acceptance of totalitarian behavior by managers in the workplace, to cite only two
of many examples). But 200 years ago it was indeed the best
show in town; and even if we haven't lived up to our potential,
we've helped the world understand the need for and effectiveness of democracy (sometimes even—as in the case of economic
competition with Japan—perhaps to our detriment).

What we will have to see, in fact—as we embark on the next
10,000 years of civilization—is the further implementation of
global democratic practices. Efforts to create a world development and a new world must incorporate democratic practices as
a norm of the world community.

While I do wish that the United States in its present state of
evolution could be the leader in this process (and I am working
to see that it can yet be), the country is actually in a precarious
position to provide such leadership. For in reality, and despite
our own conventional wisdom, it is becoming ever more apparent that we in the United States have created and promoted
an increasingly rigid class separation. We may believe in the
Horatio Alger myth that any man can become a king, but it has
always been impossible for every man to do so. In contrast, the

Japanese and the Europeans—both with some 2,000 years of historical experience—know this already. It may turn out that, in the end, they are more democratic then we can ever be, for their myths are more reality based.

According to a poll conducted by *Newsweek*, 70% of Europeans believe that there is a class system in their respective countries, and that the only way it can be destroyed is to attack it continuously by soaking the rich for taxes. At the same time, the European governments—run by parties representing the rights of the proletariat—are beefing up their educational systems for all the classes so that distinctions based on educational differences will become less significant. This may make it difficult for those Europeans who somehow manage to become rich—when they try to hire maids or a handyman, for instance. But it does certainly work to reduce class distinctions. It's a curious thing to see ads in the Iowa newspapers nowadays, looking for local girls to be nannies in England. With workers now represented on the boards of directors in European companies—and with true democracy where the people rule in terms not only of the political system but also of the economic system becoming more and more common—we must recognize a democratic process evolving in Europe that is quite different from the one here in the United States.

In contrast, people in the United States—and amazingly this is supported by those who are least likely to benefit—have come to believe that the rich should not be soaked. (Only 10% of voters in 1988 classified themselves as liberals.) After all—the thinking must go—when it's your own turn, you won't want to be soaked any more than those who were rich before you. Of course, few of these people—unless they happen to buy the right lottery ticket—will ever enjoy the advantages they cede to the rich. Given the realities of U.S. history, it is truly amazing that this has come about.

The current trend of conservative/antidemocratic behavior in our political and cultural system, if continued, will take us ever further from our democratic traditions—weak as they always have been in the economic sphere. Management behavior, for example, has been predominantly autocratic throughout U.S. history, and remains so. To some extent one could say that we have been allowed to select democratically the autocratic means by which we make a living. One may therefore conclude that we are in fact a class society; and ironically, it is the national desire to "make it" economically that is doing us in democratically. In any case, the weaknesses and limitations in our democratic values and institutions may inhibit our ability to lead a world-development effort, at least as a unified nation. On the other hand, the country is so big that, even if only 5 percent of the population were to become directly involved, this would still amount to 13 million people—and that's a lot of people.

Noam Chomsky condemns even more strongly the political institutions of this country. He sees an actual collusion between government and industry that is controlling the people under the veneer of democracy. Dissenting opinion is eliminated not by rifle squad, but by exclusion from access to information and communication with other like-minded people—who as a group could form a countervailing influence capable of changing the direction of the two controlling parties.[6]

To a certain extent, this controversial position of Chomsky's is accurate. It explains on the one hand how the likes of an Iran-Contra deal could be carried out—by the exclusion of information even from leaders of Congress—but it largely ignores on the other hand the countervailing "organic" organizational networks such as the anti–Vietnam War movement that have arisen in the past and are capable of arising again. For example, it could be argued that the reason we got an Iran-Contra scandal in the first place was the grass-roots antiwar clamor against involvement in Central America—which led to the Reagan Administration's covering up. The government knew that the majority of the nation's citizens did not support its maneuvers there.

While I must acknowledge that Chomsky's position is an all too accurate presentation of the subversion of the democratic process in this country, I want to believe that the situation began to change in the last years of the 1980s. As we take charge of our politicians and government, maybe we can at last substantiate the myth of democracy that was established in the early nineteenth century, but that largely failed us in the twentieth. Being one American who wants to see the myth debunked and a real U.S.-initiated democratic leadership I am concerned about the way we go about this. We can't rely on the political institutions as now defined (which, more and more so, operate independently of the will of the people), but must act through people–organized and controlled volunteer organizations (which initiate and carry out efforts that could never have been conceived by the political institutions of the country, due to their shortsightedness. We might then be able to take charge and create volunteer-controlled, grass-roots organizations capable of creating a new world. The role of the volunteer may well be a pivotal element in effecting those initiatives that will really help people throughout the world.

## THE POLITICAL SYSTEM TODAY AND THE GENERATION OF TOMORROW'S LEADERS

In terms of the United States' providing democratic leadership as the world community works out a development strategy, what the class system is doing to U.S. children—40% of whom were said to be living in poverty in the late 1980s—can only bode an uncertain future.

For it is our children who will ultimately save us. They will be the major players in any world development as they grow up; and we might therefore presume that they ought to be conditioned to see themselves as members of a global community, with a basically egalitarian outlook and responsibility in sharing the global resource pie.

But what has been done to our kids is no less than criminal. As the prominent pediatrician Barry Brazelton indicates, in today's two-income home, children get the short shaft.[7] Employer institutions do not, for the most part, provide a leave of absence for the parents of newborns so that the imprinting process can be carried out properly in the first few critical weeks. Having all but failed on that score, our society then responds inadequately to the need for available—or, more accurately, affordable—and decent child-care facilities. (The United States is the only developed county that does not have government-subsidized child care.) Parents more often than not end up putting their children in what amounts to a warehouse (or worse, a torture chamber). Once again the children miss out on the very important verbal and physical attention necessary to produce a self-assured individual who is able to connect with the outside world.

Our antichildren government and institutions will pay us back (and already have) with dull, apathetic adults whose constructiveness in the modern science-based economy is limited. In 1989 the new president talked about changing all that, but as the 1990s approach no significant effort has yet been made. Nobody really knows for sure what we can expect from the long-term effects of such a childhood. It's difficult to show a direct correlation between the large numbers of bored, anomic, drug-using children that our society produces today and their upbringing, but—given that the lack of attention to childhood imprinting by the two-income family has been going on for some twenty years—one's suspicion that there is a connection between the two is a pretty safe bet.

But even if those first childhood years haven't attended to properly (although most parents now—especially those who are not hampered by being members of the underclass—are involved to some extent in developing viable infant- and child-care alternatives, as well as pressuring the government to support their development, there are still things that can be done in the classroom to compensate for some of the preschool deficiencies—contingent, of course, on having teachers capable of doing the job. The training of the next generation of teachers is in itself another institutional problem that the country is having to come to grips with. And the priority must be with those who are teaching kindergarten through sixth grade, for they will be primarily responsible for shaping the attitudes and values that will be carried into the twenty-first century in support of world development. (After the sixth grade, a student's plasticity is much more limited.)

One may well ask whether the teaching of values is not the responsibility of the family (and in fact, to avoid lawsuits from parents, most school systems today do stay away from the values and focus only on the mechanics of the various disciplines). The answer is yes. But most U.S. families are clearly not providing the kind of value training necessary for a global awareness that will allow us, as a species, to survive the danger decades of the next fifty years. Like it or not, the schools are probably our only avenue to achieving this awareness.

This need not be yet one more antidemocratic process (as Chomsky might see it): The school systems have long played that role. In the nineteenth century and for too much of the twentieth, the primary role of the U.S. educational system was to provide the basic training and discipline needed to turn the majority of students into productive workers in a primarily labor-intensive economic system that had little relationship to the global community. It worked pretty well until the late 1930s. The first failure occurred when the population's basic ignorance compounded the tragedy of the Great Depression. The voters elected just as ignorant congressmen, who could not understand the global interdependency that was manifesting in national economic distress. Their counterproductive legislation in the form of the Smoot-Hawley tariff bill is a case in point. Had the people in that Depression electorate been taught in their education years to understand the complex, interdependent nature of a world economy, it is possible that they would have elected officials who would have created the legislation that could have controlled the excesses of that global catastrophe. And if we don't improve our understanding of global mechanics soon, we may well repeat the experience.

To pursue a truly sustained world development, there must be a widespread change in the values and understanding relayed to the children who will, as adults, initiate and carry out that process. The schools are the fastest way to accomplish that end. It can be done, and already has been—on a limited basis. One historical example was the progressive education system of the late 1940s in California, which did indeed produce students who had a global understanding (and which I will discuss in detail in Chapter 7).

Consequently, a major element in creating a new world will be the training and conditioning of our children to both understand and value the need for a global interaction with one's brothers and sisters. We'll need people who have an internalized desire to help others in a global system, and who will therefore voluntarily do so.

That shouldn't be so very controversial, for it is asking no more than that we produce a generation of people who behave in the finest tradition of the Christian majority who make up this country. Helping others—doing unto others as you would have them do unto you—is a solid part of how we view ourselves, and it is a value and sense of purpose that can be reinforced in the classroom. Hopefully, that early conditioning will follow people throughout their lives. The golden years may be the best time of all for those who engage in world-development activities, because of the health advantages that come with utilizing their life skills voluntarily for others.

## VOLUNTEERISM AND THE GOLDEN YEARS

The recommendation to do volunteer work for others in one's golden years is consistent with at least one occidental version of the stages of human life—Dante's, to be specific. In *Creative Mythology*, as Joseph Campbell describes it thus:

*Adolescence*, the first stage, . . . extends to the age of twenty five. . . . The second portion is that of *Mankind* (in the more enlightened, less sexist world of today, Dante most likely would have called it *personkind* acknowledging that women, being more than vessels to perpetuate the species, march through these states right alongside their man), . . . twenty-five to forty-five. Its proper virtues are temperance, courage, love, courtesy, and loyalty, its aim is achievement. The final stage is to be of *usefulness*.[8]

This final stage—usefulness; serving the human community—extends from the age of forty-five to seventy, and contrasts with certain oriental notions of the same age where the objective is to retreat into the forests, to make the final transition of returning to God. From my own point of view, we only return to God by doing something in those last years that justifies the journey through life we were lucky enough to have received.

In any case, it's not improper to say that Dante described a time when (at least in western societies) it is a natural purpose of each person's life to serve others—to be useful to the community. Certainly, volunteerism is one way to achieve that final stage of usefulness.

The major task will be to produce the necessary number of people who have these personal values when they reach person- hood. To be sure, even now there are many who have reached that state on their own—through whatever personal journey brought them there. But we will need millions of people—not thousands—to reach that state if we are to talk seriously of a vol- unteer solution to world development. This means that, while we can start the process with the thousands of people who have reached personhood on their own, we will have to institute some means by which we can perpetuate the creation of this kind of person. In other words, it means directing the education of our children to produce the kind of person that the world now needs. We can make it, with a little bit of luck; but we will have to consider implementing some of the mechanisms and technol- ogies presented in the following chapters.

## CONCLUDING REMARKS

Joseph Campbell wrote of the role mythologies play in the development of a people, and how these myths then guide a country or a civilization in its journey through history. One myth we carry with us in the United States is that, because we rep- resent the cradle of democracy (being the first country based on the principle of majority rule), we are 100-percent democratic in the practice of all our primary institutions. This is not at all true. But fortunately, our system—flawed as it is—does allow us to examine and change it (even if we have to scream in the ears of our politicians to accomplish that). And who knows?—with a little luck and volunteer effort, we may someday more closely approximate the myth in our day-to-day behavior.

In an interview shortly before his death in 1988, Campbell touched only ever so briefly on one problem that may face the development of a new world. He lamented that there is no mythology to serve as a guide—a beacon—for the development of a global community.[9]

But the relevant question here is, Do we really need a global myth to guide us in kicking off roughly the next 10,000 years of civilization? And if we do, what sort of myth should it be? A myth of manifest destiny in colonizing the solar system and ultimately the galaxy? The closest approximation we have to anything like that is in the writings of certain science-fiction novelists, who effect only a very small part of the global population.

I cannot think of any myth relating to global cooperation; societies typically create myths that put their own country to advantage. And this is probably a good thing, too—for in the recent past there has been plenty enough to do in debunking the myths of nations. (One of the most obvious and expensive efforts was World War II—debunking the myth of the Germans as the master race). Besides, if we create myths that make us masters of the universe, what will the Martians think?

I should think that Campbell himself would find it fortunate that there are no global myths to correct or debunk. Most likely, such a myth would ultimately be distorted to the advantage of one Earth group over another.

Quite simply, then, if we are to find the pathway to a new world, it must be through the power of science and through the basic human behavioral reality that we have an underlying predisposition to help our fellow humans—even if, for the most part, this predisposition has been suppressed by the institutional processes that our myths and ways of organizing ourselves have produced up to this time. Noam Chomsky may be more pessimistic about the need of men and women to be concerned about their fellow human beings. But he would surely agree that, to resolve the overwhelming global problems of the twenty-first century, something other than what has been practiced in human communities up until now will have to occur. I submit that the rationality of good will is just lying there in full sight. With a little luck and perseverance, combined with some active volunteerism, we should be able to pick it up as we rush into the new century, and use it as our standard for a true world development.

The following chapters will outline how an integrated volunteerism can provide a primary vehicle for that world development, and the creation of a new world.

## NOTES

1. Poughkeepsie *Journal*, January 1, 1989, p. 1B.
2. See A. Jedlicka, *Organizational Change and the Third World* (New

York: Praeger, 1987), for an exposition on the difficulties of changing organizations and the bureaucrats that run such organizations.

3. E. Growald, and A. Luks, "The Healing Power of . . . ", *American Health* (March 1988).

4. "The Daughters of Eve," *NOVA*, PBS Television, June 15, 1988.

5. B. F. Skinner, *Beyond Freedom and Dignity* (New York: Alfred A. Knopf, 1974), p. 203.

6. Noam Chomsky interview on *A Conversation with Bill Moyers*, PBS Television, September 20, 1988.

7. Barry Brazelton interview on *A Conversation with Bill Moyers*, PBS Television, October 2, 1988.

8. Joseph Campbell, *The Masks of God: Creative Mythology* (New York: Viking, 1968). Emphasis added.

9. Joseph Campbell interview on *A Conversation with Bill Moyers*, PBS Television, January 10, 1988.

# TWO

# Bureaucratic Organizations Will Not Create a World Development

## ON THE HOPELESSNESS OF TRADITIONAL BUREAUCRATIC MEANS

In world-development circles, the conventional wisdom says that to affect events on a macro scale one must enlist the skills of large international change institutions. Supposedly, only they have the skilled people who know how to do the job right. However, such institutions are supported and funded by donor political systems, whose motives (and expectations of reciprocity, such as access to raw materials and markets) are *always* directed to achieving more than the mere lifting up of humanity. I recall a young Peace Corps worker returning from field duty who said that a local embassy person he worked with had told him that the only purpose of developmental aid is to open up markets in the host country.

To put it more bluntly, institutional aid to Third World development exists to curry the favor of recipients. I have my own tales to tell in this regard. As a young, reasonably sensitive graduate student working on a short-term international assignment, I was thoroughly apprised of reality by a drunken OAS official at a cocktail party, who spent much of the evening informing me that international aid and bureaucrats had "nothing to do with helping people." Actually, his comments weren't all that devastating to me. I had already experienced a two-year tour of Peace Corps duty in Bolivia—this in the 1960s when the U.S. government was essentially buying out the Bolivian government so it could bring in the Green Berets to help capture poor old Che Guevara and his small band of misfits. Still, I felt somewhat like the student in the movie *The Graduate*, being told by a similarly drunk businessman that the future is plastics.

I see that same buying-out process occurring today in Honduras—a country that, prior to its recent strategic importance in the propaganda war against Nicaragua, was virtually ignored by the U.S. government. Now one finds several multimillion-dollar development projects in agriculture and rural education being initiated by the United States, and people like me being asked to staff those projects. This amounts to a new form of banana republic, where a country—rather than a business consortium—buys another country to better serve its manifest destiny.

In terms of creating effective programs that can really help people, this causes some serious problems, for the recipient of such temporary largesse knows that it is temporary and may in turn be less than honorably motivated in accepting these cynically offered gifts. But even if the host country is motivated to do the best with what is offered while it lasts, the biggest barrier to carrying out an honest effort turns out to be the bureaucracies administering the program (on both sides of the relationship), for they too often make a mockery of any underlying concern to satisfy basic human needs. This is what my OAS official was talking about, it's essentially important to understand how bureaucratic line institutions affect the development process.

To begin with—just as the OAS official said—bureaucracies are less concerned with satisfying their ultimate clients (the people in the bush), and primarily concerned with maintaining their position, power, and control of the budget. Consequently, while lip service may or may not be paid to involving the ultimate recipients' needs and feelings in the decision-making process, this is really not a concern of those in charge. It is the unabashed position of the bureaucracies that they know what's best for the people they serve.

Take, for example, the Zambian agriculture project described by some of its administrators at a rural-development conference that I attended recently in England.[1] The Zambian presenters talked about the childishness of the farmers and how it had become absolutely necessary to impose bureaucratic control over the project's recipients because they were much too ignorant to handle things on their own. This attitude of "father knows best" was even more strikingly disturbing because it was not at all unlike the views expressed by the colonial administrators who once shouldered the "white man's burden." Here the men shouldering the burden—and doing a terrible job of it—were black. But the same generalized insensitivity to recipients' concerns as had been expressed by both my student's embassy official and my OAS official were restated in no uncertain terms by the Zambian speakers. Once again the focus was on facilitating the effectiveness of the professional bureaucratic process, and not necessarily on satisfying the clients' basic needs.

One major problem is that too much of development work uses nineteenth-century administrative procedures. Such management may be somewhat effective, but only when the bottom-line strategy is the use of power backed by military force (such as in Zambia) and when there is no particular concern over whether there be a body count ultimately, or the size of the body count. This was dramatically illustrated in China in June 1989 when student demonstrators against (among other things) the corrupt bureaucracy were murdered and incarcerated. But today's Third World countries need to go beyond such a primitive means of administering their development. The body count is now being scored by the same people who originally overthrew the white (or white-run) oppressors—past masters in the science of producing body counts. In the long run particularly, such a management strategy proves itself to be dysfunctional.

On the other hand, consider another development example. Look at China before the June 1989 massacre, during those ten or fifteen years when its rigorous maintenance of a bureaucratically directed and controlled economic system was being changed to a decentralized, client-involved free market system. The gains in productivity and in consumer spending power during that period were quite dramatic, and served as a lesson to all developing countries. Yet too many of China's Third World

brothers maintain their bureaucratically dominated change institutions (even in some of the democracies), inhibiting their
effectiveness with the most basic and universal target of
change—the poor people of their respective countries. In other
words, regardless of political ideology—be they capitalist, Marxist, or socialist—bureaucracies are the enemies of the people,
and they do not operate in the interest of improving mankind.[2]
Unfortunately, in the case of China, it looks as though the bureaucracy ultimately won out. If we are to be serious about
creating a world development, we will have to replace the ignorant, insensitive domination of development by bureaucracy
with a people-oriented, person-to-person approach. Volunteers
serving others provide the grass-roots approach that is needed.
How it can be effected will be explained in subsequent chapters.

## WHY BUREAUCRATIC ORGANIZATIONS WILL FAIL

Bureaucratic organizations and the way they operate are quin-
tessentially a function of their environment. That is to say, they
can be benign or evil, efficient or inefficient. It is all a matter of
their surroundings.

Thus, in a Third World country such as India, national bureaucratic agencies that are ponderous, inefficient, and increasingly irrelevant continue to function because they are part of the
government, which has too much vested interest in the status
quo to do anything else. But local governments in India—such
as the state of Kerala, which has basically gone it alone and
created its own people-based and -controlled bureaucracy—
operate in contrast to the nation-state. The almost town-meeting
nature of development in Kerala is based on the policy that its
administrators be specifically controlled by the participants they
serve. Kerala has been able to figure out people-based ways to
get things done that could not have been accomplished by the
national government—and at considerably less cost. Consequently, Kerala—unlike Zambia—has shown that bureaucracies
can indeed be made efficient, given the will to control them and
make them perform the service function for which they were
developed.

However, the Keralas of the world are rare. In our imagining of a serious world-development effort, we will have to think of ways to eliminate or minimize the control and domination exercised by bureaucracies. Life is too short to consider reforming all the world's bureaucracies into democratic, people-focused institutions. Volunteerism is much more amenable to the establishment of an equitable world development and a new world. Volunteer efforts do not possess the inherent institutional failings of bureaucracies.

## HISTORIC AND PREHISTORIC REASONS FOR BUREAUCRATIC INSENSITIVITY

Bureaucratic inefficiency has been with us for a long time; its origin could even possibly be prehistoric—lying somewhere in our ancestral transition from the paleolithic to the neolithic society. Bureaucracies may in fact be still behaving in a manner that was created by Cro-Magnon man.

In now creating a true world development, concerned citizens of all nations should take a look at how we as a species have developed our institutions, and the way that we have historically and presently controlled each other. The picture that emerges is not pleasant, for it shows our lack of progress and the basic inhumanity that became institutionalized some 10,000 years ago when Homo sapiens transcended into early civilized man.

Thus, in resolving the present global human condition, we may have to take a step backward—a step that will allow us to reincorporate some of the small-group behavior of earlier mankind (and as still typified in the few remaining hunter-gatherer societies). The idea is to produce a cooperative, more nurturing and interactive behavior between members of a given community—no matter how technically sophisticated that community may be.[3]

Richard Leakey traces the origins of bureaucracy (although he doesn't express it exactly that way) to the ancestral destroying of the sense of community that existed in paleo-man on the way to becoming organizational man. This was an unfortunate prerequisite to civilization.[4]

The archaeological evidence for Leakey's view is found in a

large cave in southern Spain that apparently served as an annual or semiannual gathering place for Cromagnon man. As this cave (easily the size of several large shopping malls) was excavated in the 1930s, it became apparent that the area was sectioned into specific departments for various craft enterprises (arrowheads in one department; spears in another; jewelry in yet another). A kind of department-head organization must also have developed: In one part of the cave, people apparently congregated in such a way that a large number of them faced a small group, and the people in this small group were in turn facing the large group—just as supervisors do when they address a body of people. Nobody will ever know exactly what went on in that cave, but—given the present state of human nature—it is reasonable to assume that it housed some kind of centralized direction and control. Perhaps it was a scene of managers speaking to department heads of the assorted "factories," or chiefs telling their lieutenants what had to be done in the day-to-day operation of their tribes, or managers/chiefs consolidating their relationships with other managers/chiefs and lieutenants for whatever large-scale endeavor they might have had in mind. In any case, something was going on in the way of centralized control over people that is really no different from what is done today, for there was someone controlling and directing and others who followed. And no doubt there was a prototypical bureaucratic tendency to screw up the process.

In regard to early human societies, then—given the relative lack of sophistication in persuading large masses of people to accept control and direction (although in the micro level of the hunter-gatherer society, early man's behavioral controls were indeed quite sophisticated), and based on very early written evidence of war, force, and coercion—it is safe to say that hegemony was established primarily through the use of force.

We have not really changed much from those cave days, and most of today's bureaucratically controlled state organizations still use force as a means of getting people to do what the state wants. In the bad old days of the Soviet Union, for example, the penalty for noncompliance with the bureaucratic state could mean a firing squad or a vacation in the Gulag Archipelago. In

China during June 1989, it meant gunning down students. And that is really no different from an Auchiellian hand axe to the chest: It may be the substitution of an improved technology, but it's the same old mind-set. Even where bureaucracy-dominated government doesn't use overt force, such as in the United States, there are control techniques like the blacklist, the one-sided evaluation, and unilateral dismissal that play the same role—the damage in this case being psychological, rather than physical.

The predominant problem, therefore, in producing a world development is the fact that bureaucratically controlled state organizations and the operating philosophy behind them have not really changed (despite Max Weber's elucidation) since the days when they were first developed. Bureaucracies will always serve their own needs when push comes to shove (as the Chinese students can testify). And quite possibly, the basic worthlessness of the professional bureaucrat was already established early on, in those prehistoric meeting places among the caves of southern Europe.

## THE WORTHLESSNESS OF THE PROFESSIONAL BUREAUCRAT

One fundamental reason for the failure of international efforts to develop the economies and uplift the downtrodden masses of the Third World (aside from the issue of strings attached) has to do with the international alignment or sympathies of nations. A country that is in one of the superpowers' political camps and supports its political ideas or is vital to its national interest (such as providing a supply of strategic minerals) will receive from the superpower some kind of developmental aid, even if that country is a human rights violator. Such moral failure is compounded by the fact that bureaucrats and bureaucratic systems are just not very good at doing a job that really helps people. One has only to consider the mismanaged U.S. effort to help its own downtrodden masses through the Great Society programs created during the Johnson Administration of the mid-1960s.

Look at some of the accomplishments of the Great Society.

There were successes such as the development of food stamps, the Women and Infant Care (WIC) supplemental food program for low-income pregnant women, and to a lesser extent some of the Job Corps training programs (which—the sceptics claimed—seemed most effective in preparing undereducated black men to pass the "intelligence" tests that would permit them to enter the armed forces and the Vietnam War). These three government actions—it may be fairly argued—were successful because they fit the most basic requirement for a bureaucratic solution: administrative simplicity. Developing an effective food-stamp program, for instance, is largely a matter of finding out who is eligible according to some predetermined list of criteria, putting those eligible people on the list, and following up with a monthly check. Yet even so simple a bureaucratic procedure can be remarkably bungled. One Washington insider estimated to me (during one of my consulting jobs, helping to improve a similar check-sending bureaucracy of the government) that there is a consistent 20-percent minimum error in carrying out that function.

Nevertheless, these are indeed relatively simple and straightforward bureaucratic procedures. Consider the problematic nature of a really complex social issue—such as identifying the disaffected poor, targeting the right skill training to integrate them effectively into the economic mainstream, and then changing the attitudes of everyone else in society toward them. It was just these very complex developmental issues that were tackled by the numerous bureaucracies of the Office of Economic Opportunity (OEO) created in 1965. The developmental issues were never effectively resolved. In fact, several studies in the early 1980s concluded that the targeted group of people was no better off then it had been before the OEO effort, despite the billions of dollars spent on its programs. Bureaucrats, however, benefited during the time of OEO, as new government departments and their staffs burgeoned.

Virtually all such agencies are gone now—victims of the Republican party and its budget-paring maneuvers. And—I should add—rightly so, since they did a very poor job of solving social problems. However, despite their overall ineffectiveness, more recent studies show the alarming effect on the low-income groups that the Great Society programs tried to help as what did work was taken way. For example, the United States now ranks nineteenth in world infant-mortality statistics and is "rising" to an all-time low for that distinction, in large part because the government programs that were providing infant food supplementation and prenatal care have been eliminated without replacement by any significant volunteer effort (although musician Paul Simon's free, mobile medical-care operation in New York is one example of how effective the volunteer alternative can be). It is highly unlikely—given the nation's significant budget deficit and the population's general reluctance to accept greater taxation—that the bureaucratic expansion characteristic of the 1960s will ever reoccur. And as stated above, this is just as well, considering its overall ineffectiveness. I would opt instead for a federal/state-supported volunteer system focused specifically on human needs—eliminating the controls and ineffectiveness of professional bureaucratic methods. Look at what church groups and food banks do with minimal money and no professional bureaucracy and you then have an idea of what can happen when committed people work directly on satisfying basic human needs.

My own awareness of bureaucratic ineffectiveness began some years ago when I was recruited as a possible director for one of the last OEO programs. Inviting myself to be a participant observer in the selection committee's other administrative activities, I was allowed to sit in on committee discussions without undergoing a formal introduction. So consequently, the majority of its members had no idea who I was, and behaved in their normal manner.

To make a detailed story short, that evening and the next few days were spent discussing ways in which the organization's budget could be expanded, how it could more effectively impose its wishes on competing government agencies, and how its people could slit the throats of certain OEO interagency competitors—who were rank amateurs, I was told.

All of this may have a familiar ring to it, for private organizations commonly engage in dirty pool to maximize their control and position. The significance in this case is that this was a federal agency whose primary purpose was to service the needs of rural low-income Americans. Basically, very little discussion took place concerning how those people could be best served;

and when clients were mentioned, it was more often than not in a denigrating and pejorative manner. As it turns out, this preoccupation with bureaucratic activities and control—rather than a focus on effective service to people—was all too often the case among OEO bureaucracies throughout the 1960s and early 1970s.

I mention this story now without a sense of anger, however, for—by definition—professional bureaucrats can be expected to behave that way. It is—after all—the essential qualities of pettiness, power play, and worthlessness that we mean when we call them "bureaucrats." We cannot expect them to be anything else, no more than we would expect a leopard to lose its spots. The point to be realized is that if we are looking for change to occur on a macro scale then we cannot expect professional bureaucrats and bureaucratic organizations to do a good job. Volunteers are more cost effective and more personally satisfying to the people they serve because they do not work for money, power, or control of other bureaucrats and bureaucratic organizations. Volunteers are in the enviable position of being able to work for one central objective, which is to serve people most effectively without serving hidden agendas. In an era of limited budgets, there is also the advantage that volunteers work for free. Consequently, if we would talk about an effective international development effort, then we must talk about incorporating the unique strengths of the volunteer organization and must look for ways to avoid bureaucracy-dominated development approaches. I will further specify my thoughts on this subject in Chapters 5 and 6.

## THE NEED FOR EFFECTIVE COLLABORATION BETWEEN NATIONS

That there will have to be greater collaboration and communication between nations in an organizational and operational format that will facilitate the process of international development is obvious. Exactly how to construct such a global (non-bureaucratic) structure that all cultures and countries can interact with is not quite so easily seen.

One major problem is that not all countries operate from the same framework of rationality. In the case of Iran during the

1980s, for instance, the political MO looked like nothing short of insanity. However, viewed from an historical perspective—the fifteenth century, when the last of the great Moslem-Christian wars took place—Iran's behavior seems not quite so crazy. The problem in terms of world development is how to merge such extremely different political philosophies into an acceptable means of working together. What can be done to transcend the significant differences in the way nations and their bureaucratic systems function, to produce a more workable international system?

Modifying each of our various national bureaucratic systems to this end would be no easy task, but at least one megacountry—the Soviet Union (and to a lesser extent the other Warsaw Pact countries)—seems to be trying. Of the two largest monoliths of bureaucratic power (the U.S. and the Soviet)—both with their unique bureaucratic styles and their political spheres throughout the world—one of them, the Soviet, is now changing dramatically, at least on the surface.

It is fortunate, in my view of what the world should be, that the Marxist or Soviet format of heavy centralized planning has failed; it shows that a less than adequate input of the people affected by development schemes will greatly handicap the chances of successfully carrying out change. At a conference recently held in Omaha, one Soviet embassy representative indicated that this lack of involvement by the target groups themselves consistently emerges as a reason why the Soviet bureaucracies have failed. People want to participate in the process of developing how their lives will be controlled.[5]

The very fact that the Soviet system itself is now conducting *glasnost* and publicly examining an increased individual involvement in its human-services sector is proof to the world that an overbearing centralized bureaucracy is not conducive to effective change.

Yet too often overlooked is the fact that, while the United States has long led the world in the democratic tradition, our industrial and governmental bureaucratic systems are almost as centrally autocratic as the Soviet political bureaucracies have been. In fact, one of the worst offenders of workers' rights has been the publishing unit of the Library of Congress—which pays

minimum wages, will not allow unions, and requires its employees to work in deplorable sweatshop conditions.[6] While we
may not execute dissenters or condemn them to the Gulag, we
do blacklist or otherwise terminate deviants who do not fit the
bureaucratic structure. Since such treatment eliminates what
produces a person's self-esteem in society, it might as well be
physical annihilation.

In any case, considering all the evidence against it, how could
we ever have thought that the heavily centralized and bureaucratized international-development organization (in contrast to
the highly mobile, highly personal volunteer organization)
would lead to effective world development? The answer, of
course, is that we no longer can. Yet for too many countries, the
role                                                         model for developmental change is still based on old nineteenth-
century bureaucracies that, within their respective political
spheres of influence, have been shown to be ineffective. Look at
the very different experiences of two developing countries: Zambia (discussed earlier in the chapter), and Nicaragua—both
Marxist in their basic political philosophy.

## NICARAGUA AND NONBUREAUCRATIC DEVELOPMENT

Nicaragua, in contrast to Zambia, was significantly changing
its bureaucratic institutions and operations throughout the
1980s. This resulted in a kind of internationalized development
process (with news reports being commonly aired on our three
major television networks), and included a curious willingness
to allow U.S. church groups to wander about the country doing
various good works. The Catholic Church further complicated
things, imposing its moral order on the regime's control efforts—
no less than by having the pope publicly chew out President
Daniel Ortega. When the primary representative of God on Earth
criticizes the leader of a Catholic country, that leader had better
think twice about how he is serving his people.

Consequently, Nicaragua's bureaucratic control has never
been firmly entrenched. On the one hand, bureaucrats ration
the amount of food, and those who do not support the government get little. On the other hand, beyond the control of the

state bureaucracy, free-ranging U.S. church groups establish their own grass-roots agricultural programs and food banks.[7] Then too, in response to an upsurge in religious concerns, the Marxist state was flexible enough to let its publishing bureaucracy go into the Bible production business, thus satisfying a specifically expressed need of the people. As it happens, this is one of the few state operations that actually makes a profit.

So we see both flexibility and inflexibility. Some may say it's just that this is Latin America and that Latin countries have been big on inconsistent ideology. I prefer to see it as an affirmation that grass-roots, personalized development efforts work best. The Nicaraguan government has been flexible enough to see the advantages of this method, and to allow it to exist rather than clamping down or pushing it into a rigid state bureaucracy. This is all very unlike Zambia, where line bureaucracies have tightly controlled all development efforts according to nineteenth-century scientific management practices.

Again, the stereotype that regards Latin Americans, and Nicaraguans specifically, as emotional persons incapable of sticking to anything so methodical as a consistent set of policies and bureaucratic procedures is not at all true. Nicaragua represents the first "people's" revolution to have gone public, allowing international volunteer organizations as well as the media to work with it as it institutionalizes its development systems. It's a revolution in which, through the new international communication networks (about which more in Chapter 6), volunteers of nongovernmental organizations (NGOs) have been able to interact with, participate in, and ultimately change the policies of the government. There have been NGO volunteers of all backings and persuasions in Nicaragua, from conservative factions to humanitarian causes.

But before going any further, let me briefly explain that this isn't the first time the United States has been in Nicaragua. U.S. Marines occupied the country in the late 1920s and the 1930s, and created the ruling Somoza dynasty, which remained faithful to the United States until Anastasio Somoza Debayle was overthrown in 1979. In fact, the Sandinista government gets its name from a 1930s revolutionary by the name of César Sandino who allegedly met his demise through the intrigue of the U.S. government and its ambassador to Nicaragua (a side of the FDR administration that is conveniently left out of our school books). The fact that this is not at all common knowledge with us illustrates the fact that governments prefer to hide their own indiscretions and, to the extent possible, leave their citizens ignorant of certain histories.

From the start of the Sandinista takeover, one major fundraiser for the Nicaraguan government has been the volunteer, U.S. Catholic–dominated Quest for Peace (QPO) organization, which collects humanitarian contributions for the Nicaraguan people.[8] By design, this was to match and exceed whatever the United States gave to the Contras. Consequently, the organization had already topped U.S. $50 million as of July 1987. Consistent with the other-directed behavior of volunteer organizations, QPO aid (in the form of food, clinics, and medical necessities) has been distributed evenhandedly throughout the country. Thus, the Nicaraguan government has been simultaneously fighting U.S. government–supported rebel forces, while allowing volunteer U.S. forces to play a substantial role in the development of its country. Such a situation could not exist in a country like Zambia where the bureaucracy rigidly controls the interface between outsiders and its citizens, and certainly would not grant such autonomy to foreigners. In Nicaragua, significantly, governmental bureaucracies did not intervene in the volunteer activities.

Obviously, geographical proximity and the network of international communications have played a significant role in the situation in Nicaragua. But nonetheless, is it not possible that this nonbureaucratic, volunteer interface in the development of the country will serve as a prototype for world development, and be even more effective in countries that are not simultaneously fighting a civil war? It certainly does seem possible. And above all—as far as the argument of this book is concerned—the situation in Nicaragua illustrates that volunteer organizations can be more effective than government bureaucracies. Now we can legitimately think in terms of a volunteer-led pathway to a new world, even in those unfortunate countries where political instability and excessive ideology complicate the development effort. Nicaragua in the 1980s, with the help of the international media, proved the point. This is particularly poignant when at the same time in El Salvador a massive bureaucratic effort sponsored by the U.S. government met with complete failure under similar conditions of protracted guerilla war. The presence there of professional bureaucrats in control of all development was the significant difference.

The lesson of Nicaragua tells us that a sustained volunteer-based and -controlled organizational effort is one step further along the path to world development than the various "band aid" concerts that we saw in the mid–1980s (although such events did recognize and utilize the key component of international media publicity, which has been so helpful to Nicaragua). The volunteer-controlled development organization is not just a short-term flash in the pan that mostly, in effect, makes record buyers feel good. It provides, rather, a long-term countervailing commitment that subverts the stultifying bureaucracy of the host country, and promotes a development more effective than the bureaucracies of host and donor countries combined.

The volunteer activity of insiders and outsiders in Nicaragua's development may well be a prototype (though not yet a perfect one) for a new world development. Hopefully, the future will bring less of the other side of Nicaragua: centralized Marxist planning; and the ineffective economic maneuvers of ex-rebels who can fight, but cannot run a country.

Development that combines the inputs of world communication and a concerned volunteer citizenry can effect change on a global basis, as well. A model employing the support network of a cross-national volunteer organization combined with the technology that makes it work will be presented in Chapter 5. But in practice—as the experience of change within nations has taught us—any such global efforts will only succeed if its participants are willing to engage in civil disobedience. And here I mean a civil disobedience that serves a higher civil order, transcending the international policies of individual countries. Volunteers must be prepared to engage in such disobedience as they develop pathways to a new world.

## ANTI–BUREAUCRATIC CONTROL—THE OBLIGATION OF CIVIL DISOBEDIENCE

What has been demonstrated by the assorted U.S. church activities in Nicaragua is that civil disobedience to the political objectives of one's own government may (if that government is behaving in a morally inappropriate manner) be totally acceptable from a global humanistic perspective (and is in fact necessary to any serious strategy for world development).

That idea is nothing new. We Americans find it articulated in the writings of Henry David Thoreau; and its first major operational follow-through appeared in the 1930s with the "Abraham Lincoln Brigade" activities of the Spanish Civil War. That group was made up of Americans who were willing to put not only their ideas—but also their lives—on the line in defense of democracy against fascism in Spain, and thousands of Americans did indeed pay the ultimate price. But the real significance of their actions in the context of world development is that these people directly disobeyed the U.S. government's policy and aided what they knew to be a just cause—which, though temporarily futile, was achieved thirty years later when the last vestige of fascism (General Franco) finally died.

The idea of a globally inspired civil disobedience cannot be overemphasized. The reality of the situation is that a true world development will always run counter to the policy objectives of some country or another. And often that country may be one's own. People must be prepared to take that risk. Actually, in the developed world civil disobedience is increasingly not so risky as it was in the 1930s, because the press—and especially television—is more effective in attracting attention to such civilian activities, and provides a kind of shield (in contrast to the fate of the Abraham Lincoln Brigade survivors, who were branded as "reds" for the rest of their working lives). For example, none of the volunteers recently working in Nicaragua has been penalized by the U.S. government, and even during the early 1970s Jane Fonda was not penalized for what amounted to her atrocious behavior toward U.S. POWs in Vietnam. In Fonda's case, this happened because of the publicity associated with her trip to Hanoi—publicity that goes with who she is. You or I would no doubt have gone to jail then, but today our chances of going to jail are remote. And media coverage in general is more inclusive. In this regard, one tactic useful to volunteer movements is the employment of retired citizens. National governments will typically avoid—like the plague—beating up seventy-year-old grandmothers, who in spirit may be more radical and dangerous than some muddleheaded twenty year old.

The willingness to defy one's own government's foreign policies (short of treason) in the final years of gunboat diplomacy (which the Soviets propose eliminating) may become a keystone of volunteer development organizations. Its ultimate effectiveness in the creation of a new world is that it allows volunteers to base their service on the merits of helping fellow human beings—and not necessarily on the values of their own countries' current administrations.

The extent to which people do currently and will in the future continue to engage in this type of civil disobedience could not have existed fifty years ago. The Abraham Lincoln Brigade and the antigovernment riots of the 1960s and early 1970s laid a philosophical groundwork for the world development of the immediate future. (Consider what may happen when the postwar Baby Boomers turn into Gray Panthers about twenty years from now, and reactivate their 1960s radicalism.) An institutionalized civil disobedience is now both acceptable and relatively risk free. But what can we look to as an organizational framework for a sustained volunteer-driven global development that is both respectable and not governmentally controlled?

The one organization that most aggressively seems to fit this form of volunteer, antibureaucrat behavior is the National Council of Returned Peace Corps Volunteers (NCRPCV). Most of its members are now in early middle age. It is a specific charge of the NCRPCV organization to serve as a watchdog on the Third World activities of U.S. government agencies, and to provide a continuous update on the political situation in countries where the returned Peace Corps volunteers served.[9] The objective of the group is to prevent abuses in the practice of official U.S. activities in the developing world. But just as importantly, one of its greatest potential contributions is to serve as a volunteer network center for globally integrated development. Thus, NCRPCV acts as a nongovernmental and countervailing organizational force that utilizes volunteer experts to further nonpolitical world-development efforts. As such, it could be the pioneer coordinating mechanism for a world development. As a nonbureaucratic development alternative, it will be used as a case example in the discussion of global volunteer organizations in Chapters 4 and 5, and will be commented on throughout this book.

## THE FUTURE OF U.S. DEMOCRACY

Sheldon Wolin holds one of the most pessimistic views around in regard to democracy in the United States and where it is going. In his view, we don't have democracy at all, because of our increasing reliance on centralized bureaucracies both in the governmental and private spheres. As a consequence of this trend, power is not really shared; equality goes down; and a blend of antidemocratic managerial practices and ideology adopted from the private corporations has infiltrated government institutions, making them more and more similar to the corporations.

Wolin feels that reliance on hierarchy and top-down decision making permeates the country so profoundly that every one of its primary institutions is antidemocratic including the school system. As a result, most Americans feel powerless; they are not allowed to become involved in the process of controlling their own lives. Their lack of participation in the country's major institutions generates a sense of futility and helplessness.

In the worst case scenario, this situation has helped to create what is now recognized as the underclass—a growing superfluous population for which there is no meaningful work (if any work at all). That this group has a problem with drugs and crime should not be surprising—especially in the increasingly unlivable U.S. cities, where class distinction is clearly defined by the various ghettos (be they white and affluent or poor and black).

Yet even Wolin feels that education still has possibilities "to ease us into a better world for ourselves and others."[10] In his estimation, the students of today never achieve a sense of empowerment because they are being deprived of the knowledge and sensibilities that come from "soft" subjects such as history and philosophy, which teach people to interpret what's happening to them and—above all—to understand power and its uses. Without this understanding, the citizen has difficulty developing personal control and an interaction with the system. She or he becomes ever more powerless and disenfranchised.

There are questions to be considered as we approach the year 2000. What kind of collective identity do we want? And how will we be affecting other societies, nations, and cultures? Next, can we use the educational system to create our desired collective identity, and produce citizens who understand themselves, their relationship to power, and their involvement with the world? And when we have that kind of citizen, will she or he be indeed able to overcome business as usual and create the new world?

The educational system could very well provide the means of developing and institutionalizing an international civil-disobedience strategy. According to the U.S. Constitution, the states and local government dictate what is taught in the school system. It would not be treason to teach our children that it is right to oppose actively and overtly the political objectives of any president, when that opposition is exercised for the greater good of humanity. The means by which this exciting prospect could be accomplished—without resort to hiring Trotskyites as teachers—will be discussed in Chapter 7.

## CONCLUDING REMARKS

This chapter has argued that a significant barrier to effective world development is the bureaucratic and political process that goes on within governments and traditional development agencies. The internal self-maintenance activities of bureaucratic agencies can essentially block any effective aid to the people that those agencies ostensibly serve. This is an all too common situation, which must be eliminated if we are serious about world development.

It is the premise of this book that one countervailing force to professional operations is the use of volunteer agencies because they rely on the altruism of the volunteer, who has nothing to gain except the feeling of satisfaction in doing something for others. This chapter has touched on the possibilities of this course of action. Developing that idea further will be the subject of the following chapter, and the major thrust of this book.

## NOTES

1. Rural Development Workshop of Iowa State University, held at Gregoynol, England, in September 1987.

2. A. Jedlicka, *Organizational Change and the Third World* (New York: Praeger, 1987).

3. Richard Leakey, *People of the Lake: Mankind and Its Beginning* (New York: Doubleday, 1978).

4. Leakey's presentation was made on the program *NOVA*, May 10, 1987.

5. Oleg Derkousky, Address to the Ninth Annual Third World Conference, Omaha, Nebraska, October 1988.

6. *CBS Evening News*, June 22, 1986.

7. R. Norland, J. Contreras, and D. Newell, "The Other Aid Network," *Newsweek*, July 27, 1987, p. 38.

8. *CBS Evening News*, June 22, 1986.

9. *National Council of Returned Peace Corps Volunteers Newsletter*, September 1988.

10. Sheldon Wolin interview on *A Conversation with Bill Moyers*, PBS Television, December 28, 1988.

# THREE

# Volunteerism: Essential to Effecting a World Development

In an age in which artificial intelligence is rapidly coming on-line, there may well be reason enough in this to fear for the future of mankind. All human beings are limited to dealing with four or five simultaneous events whenever they engage in decision making (and whatever their intentions). That has been effective enough to bring us to this point in technological development; but computers are now or soon will be able to handle ten, twenty, or even 1,000 simultaneous events. It is conceivable that there will be new and wondrous products developed that even the best computer experts will be able to use but will never really understand. That could be scary, particularly if computers happen to internalize certain malignant values not unknown among their human creators. But if the ethical values of artificial intelligence turn out to be impeccably pure, than it could usher in a time when humanity's improvement is spurred by its faithful sidekick, the computer/robot. It's amazing that the need imagined by Isaac Asimov for a law of robotics—the primary directive that robots, through any action or inaction, shall do no harm to any human being—is already being felt.[1]

Such a robotic world—and we may see the beginnings of it within a decade—can do much in the way of promoting volunteerism. With computers replacing so many decision-making and productive activities, what better to do with our newly abundant free time than to work voluntarily on spreading the benefits of the new productive systems to all of mankind. Certainly the retired (who increasingly retire at a relatively young age) and those who are well off but bored would fill the bill even now. But for the moment it is the governments of the First World—not individual volunteers—who are the mainstays of world development. Unfortunately, they are not doing the job very well.

As Chapter 2 indicated, there is reason to be pessimistic about the ability of governments and their line bureaucracies to do an effective, nonpoliticized job of helping people. One shouldn't really expect otherwise. Bureaucracies, by nature, have no theology and no real concern other than to perpetuate their own existence, even when addressing the inequalities and oppression that despoil the declining years of the twentieth century. This century has had its ironies. In its first decades, there was the "war to end all wars." And now, in its last decades, there is the comfortably telecommunicated reality that more than half of humanity goes to bed hungry every night. Millions starve to death in a world where there are many countries that pay dearly to store their surplus food production—waiting for it to go bad so that it can be justifiably thrown away allowing new surpluses to take its place! Such a century could stand to end on a more upbeat note. But the events of June 1989 in China show that the autocratic bureaucracy tradition dies hard.

If governments and traditional institutions can't do the job, then who can? Fortunately, replacing the past decade of self-centered greed (at least in the United States), there seems to be a new concern for the world condition. As indicated in Chapter 1, paleogenetic research has shown the human community to be a true brotherhood and sisterhood traceable to one woman some 200,000 years ago who is, effectively, the mother of us all.[2] Without being sentimental, then, one can honestly say that we have an obligation to help our brothers and sisters. That physical reality, combined with the new religious philosophy called "liberation theology" (which will be discussed later in the chapter), provides a nice rationale—a setting in which to activate volunteerism as a mechanism for changing the world. Hopefully, we can reignite that idealism and spirit of volunteerism that was stirred to life in the 1960s, and was then set aside in the 1980s during our national introspection about the Vietnam adventure and what it meant to all of us. It is the veterans of the Vietnam War who have finally set us free from that prolonged era of spiritual nightmare. Their militant demand to be recognized helps us expiate our collective guilt in not welcoming them home at that time or supporting their urgent need to understand what they had been forced to do.

Paradoxically enough, the final years of the decade of the Yuppies—that 1980s-style subculture—compassion and volunteerism resurfaced, and as part of a new emphasis on networking. *Newsweek* writer Annette Miller describes how young professionals, "tired of the excesses of the Me Generation,"[3] have been searching for balance and compassion. In support of this latent volunteerism (up overall from 31 percent in 1984 to nearly 50 percent in a 1987 Gallup poll), more than 600 U.S. companies (up from 300 in 1979) now encourage their workers to become involved in community service. That service could be anything from staffing soup kitchens to taking children from welfare hotels to the circus or a museum. This is certainly good news. Moreover, there is a beneficial difference between this kind of volunteerism and the so-called starry-eyed idealism of the 1960s. That difference is pragmatism, which—combined with the organizational skills of networking—can be especially appropriate to producing a world development, and not merely a rush of good feeling.

As Annette Miller writes, an MBA style "of pragmatism and a more cost-effective approach toward helping one's fellowman" is combined in this new group of volunteers with "organizational and dealmaking skills" that can maximize the investment of time a volunteer puts into her or his good deeds. For example, "faced with the prospect of bringing Christmas to children in a New York welfare hotel, a local volunteer agency got in contact with a local corporation executive who in turn used his contacts to cut a deal with Mattel for a discount on 750 toys."[4] No matter how you cut it, a new toy (still in its original wrappings, not beat up and secondhand, will maximize the effect that a volunteer's personal attention can have on a child. While the likes of Ivan Boesky (a man who in the 1980s came to symbolize the worst in civilized human behavior because of the lectures in which he claimed that the greed of the business world is good) cut deals for themselves and their cronies, those same insider skills used legally in volunteerism can only be considered good.

And applying that pragmatism, organization, and dealmaking to world development, why can't the same be done in other countries of the world? In fact it has been done in some cases. For example, as a Peace Corps volunteer years ago in Bolivia, I was part of a group that was able to lean on a U.S. company laying down an oil pipeline in the area, and persuade it to give an hour here and there making village roads with its earthmoving equipment. The goodwill that company acquired from the project greatly exceeded its minimal cost. In an age where multinational corporations are viewed with suspicion almost everywhere they go, such low-cost, highly visible, and totally relevant actions can only help to improve the international climate.

In any case, a volunteer world-development effort must include a well-organized, dealmaking, pragmatic idealism that may or may not be supported by an underlying theological base. It must be lodged solidly in a framework of actually doing something, rather than engaging—as many of our older volunteer agencies have been—in activities that primarily make the donors feel good and pay the organization's overhead.

## VOLUNTEERISM AS A REACTION TO THE 1980s

We cannot blame the whole selfish behavioral tempo of the 1980s—the rapaciousness and the glorification of greed—on the presidential administration of Ronald Reagan. After all, the trend had already started before his arrival. On the other hand, one thing we must give Reagan credit for is that he aided the reemergence of volunteerism in his effort to take government out of the business of helping people. Who knows? We volunteers (even of a different political persuasion) may someday have to build a monument to him. Let me explain.

In 1989 I find that the evening news has just discovered the homeless, the unemployed, and those who have lost their "self-esteem." In their own way, such unfortunates are now celebrities; and the itinerant bum is often on the evening news, protesting the fact that the city is violating her or his various rights. What is efficacious about all this (for the nonbums who nevertheless have to sleep on steam vents) is that both national and international volunteerism is beginning to fill in the void created by the departure of government from the field of human services. As emphasized in Chapter 2, I would never suggest that we return to the assistance programs of the Great Society, for they largely did little but support the worthless careers of an expanded federal bureaucracy. It would be more relevant to the helping of people were the federal government to fund volunteer development organizations, both nationally and internationally. Overhead expenses could be kept to a minimum because the organizations would in fact be administered and operated by volunteers who would be paid, at most, their expenses. Another idea is to allow federal income tax deductions—say to a maximum such as $15,000—for labor in kind provided through certified volunteer organizations. This could be limited to a specific age group such as fifty-five and older, so that younger people do not end up financing their children's education through volunteer labor.

Certainly, a tax deduction for older citizen volunteers does make sense. To begin with, it would have little effect on tax revenues since most retired people pay few taxes anyway. But for those higher income ex-professionals who do pay significant taxes on their social security income, a $15,000 deduction may well provide them with the incentive to apply their skills in a volunteer capacity. Actually, there are any number of financial and social incentives that would make it particularly inviting for people to become volunteers. In a world where balanced motivation is a psychological component of being normal, volunteerism and individual income tax deductions are not incompatible.

## THE PHILOSOPHIC BASE OF VOLUNTEER ORGANIZATIONS

One significant consequence of the personal awareness trends of the late 1960s, through which many people became aware of the power of the individual (not only to understand her or his inner self, but to organize with other similarly motivated people), is that antiestablishment volunteer movements are now a part of the U.S. political scene. The original framers of the Constitution recognized that power comes from the people and created (but didn't exactly promote) a system allowing for volunteer participation. Not until recently, however, have there emerged effective groups such as Quest for Peace (the U.S. pro-Sandinista support group discussed in Chapter 2) organizing actively to offset autocratic use of power by a U.S. administration.

Let's go one step further into the philosophic underpinnings of the volunteer movement. Surprisingly perhaps, we find ourselves in the nation's business schools and discover a much taught, but too little used organizational concept. That concept can be best represented as "participative management." Basically, participative management is the joint control and sharing of power by all members of an organization in such a way that all share (more or less equally as determined by their personal desire) in the development, operation, and management of the organization's behavior. In that kind of mutually shared power arrangement, the odds are that each person will develop a strong commitment to the organization. In the case of a volunteer organization, where differentiation of status among the members is eliminated because there are no titles and no salaries (let alone a differentiation of salaries), there exists an optimum opportunity to become very much participative, and to remain satisfactorily participative throughout the life of the organization. (See Chapter 4, which provides a more analytical inquiry into the nature of participative management systems.)

The United States has played an important role in history so far as the theoretical development of participative organizational structures is concerned, but its key industries and public and private institutions have always neglected that history in conducting their own operations.

## THE HISTORY OF PARTICIPATION IN THE UNITED STATES

Despite the fact that the United States is the birthplace of participative government (at least in the representational form), the practice of our institutional management systems has really shown quite the opposite. In fact, our democratic political processes themselves have been a mixed bag. The machinations of the boss system in the nineteenth century was at best a form of benevolent dictatorship. Even in Iowa—home of the presidential caucus—there has been no long tradition of grass-roots participation in the selection of presidential candidates. It was only in 1972 that the caucus determination process was introduced there (replacing the more traditional "smoke-filled room" form of candidate selection by party honchos).

The recent history of the U.S. labor movement is even more depressing: Even as late as the 1940s, labor leaders were still being blacklisted and beaten for exercising their right to organize workers. The labor movement itself is no great shakes at promoting participation, preferring instead to establish a "dictatorship of the proletariat" whereby union members participate little in the process other than dutifully electing their representatives and paying their dues. To a large extent, employer despotism has been replaced with union despotism. The *On the Waterfront* situation is too often a reality in today's unions.[5] On the employers' side, union busting is still not giving way to a kinder, more benign form of management. New technology has introduced new forms of control: There are computer-monitored keyboards that can determine whether an operator is slacking up, and visually sensitive computer monitors that can determine whether an employee is where she or he should be at any point in time. I wouldn't be surprised to find that the implantation of cerebral electronic-punishment devices is just around the corner. Such devices might automatically administer a shock whenever the computer determines that a job is not being done properly— although this would violate Asimov's prime directive that a robot never hurt a human being.

In fact, the more you analyze the political and labor traditions of the United States, the more you realize that there has been very little self-determination or involvement of its citizens in their "democratic" processes. The inescapable conclusion from all the evidence is that we have been, and are being, heavily controlled in our work organizations as well as our political institutions. That sounds like what we were fond of criticizing in the Soviet Union, doesn't it?

Unfortunately, the long tradition of nonparticipation in our work and political institutions is now significantly hurting the country in its quest to compete internationally. We seem to be increasingly at a loss both because of our lack of a technically qualified work force and because our workers cannot participatively interact with the technological processes that produce globally competitive products.

To give one example, a Japanese company that recently built a production plant in the United States had a major problem in staffing many of its "blue-collar" positions. People with high school diplomas did not have an advanced enough math background to understand how to monitor the statistical quality-control equipment—nor in fact, did the college-trained applicants. The company finally hired engineers with graduate degrees to fill the positions. As it turns out, the Japanese blue-collar worker has to take the same curriculum in high school (algebra, geometry, trigonometry) that our college-bound students do, and receives an additional four years of technical training once she or he becomes a factory worker. But equally damaging to the United States is the news that, at least in the work environment, Japan is more democratic. It encourages the participation of lower level employees not only in the development and modification of existing systems, but also in the design of new technologies. This produces a kind of industrial volunteerism, where workers will put in extra hours and effort to promote the success of the whole organization.

By our shortsighted labor-management practices, we may well be relinquishing technological leadership to other countries—countries that fortunately are our allies (and presumably will be, at least for the near future).[6] While the end result could make us reasonably happy, that happiness may come at the expense of turning into a second-class industrial nation, relying on technology transfers from our trade partners (most likely, the Japanese). That's not such a horrible possibility: After all, the British have had to accept that position in relation to us, and they don't seem particularly down in the dumps about it. Nevertheless, some Britons probably do lament their technological dependency, just as one day we may too.

As to a technological future dominated by Japan, the Japanese author Masuda—writing on the subject of artificial intelligence, robotics, and fully automated production systems—argues that such a future can release the majority of humanity from drudgery and promote the development and enhancement of an other-directed world. He seems to suggest something rather like a global Peace Corps—where human beings do not exploit other human beings, but rather nurture each other (see Chapter 6 for further discussion). In such a world, we would have no cause to lament getting behind the Japanese because robotics can in effect eliminate the kind of economic competition that has been so wasteful, and can provide an opportunity to spread wealth to all people. Specifically Masuda sees this as

taking the form of the freedom for each of us to set individual goals of self realization which may help create a worldwide religious renaissance characterized not by a belief in a supernatural god, but rather by awe and humility in the presence of the collective human spirit and its wisdom. This would be humanity living in a symbiotic tranquility with the planet we have found ourselves upon, regulated by a new set of global values.[7]

Connecting Masuda's vision with our own strategy for a world development that relies on the volunteer kindness of strangers, this religious renaissance is bounded not by the desire to convert people, but by a secular and humanistic desire to help people so that we may all equally share in the next great adventure: mankind's venture into the cosmos (the domain of most of the original gods). To realize such a global spirit, we will have to educate our children to believe in it. This can certainly be done, and the behavioral tools to do it will be presented in Chapter 7.

In any case, such a spirit is

decidedly not an otherworldly religious spirit, which makes it different from religious passions of the past. On the contrary, it is sharply focused on this world with humans having a serious, direct, and continuous say in all matters that affect their lives. But those exercises will be characterized less by the "me first" attitude that has often prevailed in human affairs, and more by a spirit of mutual assistance toward shared goals.[8]

I suggest that volunteerism will be a key component in the development of this new "religious" spirit and mutual assistance. It matters little that the Japanese are the ones who provide the facilitating technology, because such technology will liberate us from the hedonistic values that have differentiated the cultures of the world and made them antagonistic, wasting time and energy on hostile activities against each other and preventing the creation of a global extended family.

Some may say this is all very nice, but too utopian. Such a reaction is culturally bound to the past. The new technologies are already creating a world we have never known before. With a little luck this will turn out not to be a world of the "Reeks" and the "Wrecks" as described in Kurt Vonnegut's first novel *Player Piano*, where humanity wastes its time engaged in useless, make-work corporate activities. Rather it will be a world where the spirit of other-directed volunteerism extends a First World largesse to all other cultures and peoples. One prototype for this already exists in the volunteer activities of several Christian churches.

## THE CHURCHES—VANGUARD OF THE VOLUNTEER SPIRIT

When we look at who has been leading the effort toward world development through volunteerism without political attachments, we find several Christian churches right out in the forefront (but not all of them—the younger, more immature churches such as the Mormons and some of the Christian fundamentalist offshoots still being heavily into missionary proselytizing as their contribution to a world community). Among churches such as the Methodists and various factions of the Catholic Church, some rather remarkable world-development efforts are even now taking place.

No doubt this has occurred partly because of the profound effect of what is called "liberation theology," which backs up the assertion made by the Group of 77 at the United Nations that all human beings have the fundamental right to a decent life on earth, rather than having to wait for it in the afterlife or through rebirth cycles.

There has always been a rather strong religious undercurrent within countries like the United States. And as we came out of the Yuppy decade of the 1980s, there seems to be a new interest in religion and a concern with improving the human condition. Liberation theology, with its humanistic focus, certainly fits nicely with current efforts to create a world development.

What are the essential elements of liberation theology that dovetail so nicely with volunteer development efforts? For one thing, its predominant theme is that the purpose of theology is not to convince the nonbeliever of the truths of the Christian faith, but to humanize the economic, social, and political order in which all people live. Its focus—with no apologies considered necessary—is on liberating the oppressed.[9] Probably the biggest fear that establishment theologians have about liberation theology is its supposed link to communism—which naturally means the Antichrist—for some controversial new theologians have tried to show a relationship between the writings of Marx and the early Christian writers. Actually, to extend this last point even further, one could contend that a real communist (one who doesn't get bogged down with dictatorship-of-the-proletariat theories or into paranoid, authoritarian control) is closer to a real Christian than either party dogma or the establishment of Christianity would have one believe. They both espouse the principle that the downtrodden should be helped out of misery. Call that communism or Christianity. The choice is yours.

For the Westerner concerned with where the world is going and what she or he can possibly do to help suffering humanity, a theology that considers it important to eliminate oppression and materially help one's neighbor adds a spiritual (religious) incentive to the natural urge to serve. Having a church's sanction makes the satisfaction of volunteering just that much better— providing, if nothing else, the feeling of working off a few years in purgatory.

One of the more interesting efforts in volunteer development is what the United Methodist Church has been doing. Essentially, technological cadres have been sent by the church to such countries as Nicaragua to effect a service that looks more like Peace Corps work (at least like the Peace Corps of the early 1960s, before it became heavily politicized) than like a missionary expedition. The entire focus is on disseminating ways by which people can better their standard of living, rather than improve their chances of getting into heaven. Yet, such service must be consistent with Christianity, at least in its early days before church bureaucracies took hold and started making fishers of men—rather than giving them fish. The Methodist approach provides a prototype that can be emulated by other organizations.

## INFRASTRUCTURE ESSENTIAL TO AN EFFECTIVE VOLUNTEERISM

It is significant that the Methodist individuals who participate in the mission described above are actually volunteers in every sense of the word, for they do it (unlike Peace Corps workers) without pay.[10] But another significant point is that they are not winging it alone: They have the existing church infrastructure as a support agency. That translates into a place to get mail and a place to stay without incurring any long-term expenses of a hotel room. In any macro effort at world development, one essential in enlisting volunteers is to provide a place to crash. But once that essential is provided, the cost to volunteers becomes negligible. They need only pay for their flight to the country. The food they purchase is a fixed cost that they would pay at home anyway.

Thus, infrastructure is important. It can greatly facilitate the willingness of potential volunteers who might otherwise not be able to donate their labor abroad. The same thing applies to domestic volunteers: In addition to receiving a federal tax exemption for their donated labor, they should also have a designated area that serves as a crash site whenever they work in the numerous federal facilities (old military bases, hospitals, and so forth) that could be opened up to volunteer projects throughout the country. This structural interplay between the institutions of religion and state and the private volunteer organizations will be explored in greater detail in Chapter 5.

## THE PEACE CORPS

The U.S. Peace Corps has been in existence as a volunteer organization for more than 25 years, and one might tend to think of it as a prototype for the volunteer world-development movement. Unfortunately, it is not—for in reality it is not a volunteer agency at all, but a politicized offspring of the State Department. (Look at the State Department's organizational chart, and you find little Peace Corps dangling to the side, very tenuously situated in terms of the big picture.)

In the 1960s the Peace Corps was somewhat like a volunteer agency; but even then, its workers swore allegiance to the United States (not to a world community) and were managed by line bureaucrats (many on leave from the State Department) who treated them like employees and not like volunteers. (After all, in those days Peace Corps workers were paid $80 a month, and were expected to earn it.) Speaking from personal experience, I can report that this was the cause of many discipline problems. The line bureaucrats would try to use autocratic methods of controlling the volunteers; and the volunteers would respond with abrasive countermeasures—a threat to contact their senators being their ultimate line of defense—because they viewed themselves as volunteers, not employees. The problem with the Peace Corps has always been that volunteers must be treated like volunteers and allowed to participate fully in the management and decision-making functions of the organization. Treating such people with the managerial finesse of the Ford Motor Company in its low days of the 1940s only assures that the agency will not get the best from its workers. While Peace Corps management has improved somewhat, it still retains too much of the counterproductive behavior characteristic of administration in a rigid bureaucracy.

Despite all that, there was more of a volunteer aspect to the agency in the 1960s than there is now. In my own case, I was "parachuted" (an apt expression for the Peace Corps practice of dropping people into exotic isolated places) into the fifteenth century via a village of Quechua Indians in Bolivia. And for the most part, I was left alone to forage for myself and develop my own programs. This worked out perfectly until a new field director thought that I was unprofessional and had to shape up. The conflict between myself as volunteer and the director as dictator never did work out, because to him I was a subordinate employee. I knew I was a volunteer, and thus not subject to the usual power plays and control games that incompetent bureaucrats have to rely on.

Nowadays, Peace Corps "volunteers" are screened to match positions that the "host country" specifically wants filled. In effect, the volunteer fills a predetermined niche that matches the needs of the United States and the host government. Whether the match results in satisfying the needs of the people of the country or the volunteer is basically irrelevant. With that kind of politicized line control, the Peace Corps volunteer is not a volunteer at all, but a very low paid member of the State Department bureaucracy.

Consequently, the Peace Corps is not an appropriate model for world development, for its workers are employees—not volunteers with a say in the direction of the organization they serve. What too often happens today is that people play the game as long as they can stomach it, and then quit early. Turnover is high. Fortunately, the Peace Corps now pays the flight fare of those who return early; in the 1960s it didn't.

To achieve a truly volunteer world development, we must get beyond the restrictive managerial controls that development organizations such as the Peace Corps use. But we still need the infrastructure support that makes volunteerism successful. This will be discussed in detail in Chapter 5.

## VOLUNTEERISM AND RESOURCE BASES

Certainly the Methodist volunteers mentioned in an earlier section have a theological reason for doing what they do, but— like the Yuppy volunteers also mentioned earlier—there is a pragmatic orientation to their service. Most importantly, they maintain an adequate backup to assure that what they initiate can actually be carried out and positively impact people's lives. On the other hand, the Peace Corps—which in the 1960s sustained a large bureaucracy charged with the maintenance and training of new batches of volunteers—too often then left them at assignments with no real backup institutions or in-country support. One quickly discovered that there is only so much you can do with just mud and rocks.

The Methodist volunteers, using field churches as their infrastructure base, work directly with the people they wish to affect—on a equal basis. Unlike the typical development institution, these volunteers and the people they serve are involved in a strictly egalitarian relationship whereby the "recipients" participate in the planning and follow-through of every project.

Nowadays, even the large line institutions of the international agencies have heard about the advantages of equal participation in the development of technological change programs—if for no other reason than that I have been writing and consulting for the past twenty years. But in order to maintain their bureaucratic control (which will be discussed further in Chapter 4), they more often than not leave the recipients of their change efforts out of any design and maintenance functions. Yet common sense tells us that people want to be included and involved in the process of their own changing. Furthermore, without their involvement and commitment, there is no way we can expect them to continue and maintain the technologies that are introduced. One need only look at the number of empty shells in the nation's inner-city housing to get some idea of what happens when people are helped, but not involved in the process.

The advantage of volunteerism as practiced by the various religious groups is that it provides a participative means of introducing change, a resource base, and a means of creating commitment that will sustain the technological change for the long run. To be effective, the volunteer must have access to certain institutional resources, but—above all—she or he must accept the principle that the project's beneficiaries are her or his own equal, and that their input is absolutely vital. The volunteer must be a participative manager. This is the exact opposite of the bureaucratic method, which assumes that only bureaucrats have the organizational skills to prescribe and carry out effective change.

Granted the volunteer's purity of heart, then, she or he will need linkages to support organizations that can supply additional inputs of both technology and information from other volunteers. In the twenty-first century world, these linkages will be greatly (and cheaply) facilitated by the new low-cost telecommunications grids and computer retrieval systems. Volunteerism will then be coordinated as an integrated world effort, rather than the effective but limited activities of individual do-gooders. These possibilities will be discussed further in the following chapters, particularly in Chapter 6.

## CONCLUDING REMARKS

Engulfed in a technological revolution that by the end of the twentieth century will render large numbers of superbly skilled First World workers "retired early" but with decades of productivity still before them, we have an opportunity to mobilize these people toward world development. A resource base to back up such a mobilization is beginning to be created through institutions like the churches. We could go even further and—through telecommunications technology—create global extended families committed to helping each other. At long last, we can cost-effectively become our brothers' keepers. And happily—given the underlying imperatives of human nature and the technological level we have attained—volunteerism also satisfies an essential desire for world development. To sustain that volunteerism, participative methods of organization and follow-through are critical. Participation and its relationship to volunteerism is the subject of Chapter 4.

## NOTES

1. Asimov's early writings in the 1950s contained the recurrent theme that, as robots take over mean labor, they can never rebel or hurt any human.

2. "The Daughters of Eve," *NOVA*, PBS Television, June 15, 1985.

3. A. Miller, "The New Volunteerism," *Newsweek*, February 8, 1988, p. 37.

4. Ibid.

5. *On the Waterfront* was a movie directed by Elia Kazan that depicted the corruption of longshoremen unions in the early 1950s.

6. E. Feigenbaum and P. McCorduck, *The Fifth Generation* (New York: Addison-Wesley, 1983), p. 240.

7. Ibid.

8. Ibid. p. 241.

9. Outspoken proponents of liberation theology such as Allan Boesek have repeatedly sounded this secular theme.

10. R. Norland, J. Contreras, and D. Newell, "The Other Aid Network," *Newsweek*, July 27, 1987, p. 38.

# FOUR

# Participation and Volunteerism

It is a primary philosophical base of any serious volunteer effort toward world development that equality, participation, and grass-roots organization are the key ingredients for success. Volunteers and recipients must themselves be empowered to control the process.

This has traditionally been a problem with development efforts in the Third World. Projections have been initiated, designed, and implemented—too often—without any involvement of the project recipients. The result has been—too consistently—the absence of any long-term success.

It is always convenient to blame the giver of aid—the developed countries—for improper development and follow-through in such failed efforts. And it is true that much fault does lie with the international agencies who have failed to incorporate a grass-roots, participative approach in the design of their programs. But it is equally true that the Third World governments working with these agencies also have some bearing on the effectiveness of the programs. For example, in 1989, Imelda Marcos was being criticized for misuse of development aid in the Philippines; the Honduran military was suspected of using diplomatic immunity to conduct drug trafficking; and the Nigerian military dictatorship, with its form of state capitalism, had become notorious for insisting on its due in bribes for anything done in the country—

to name but a few Third World governments. (And in June 1989, HUD officials of the U.S. government were also investigated for influence peddling, which only confirms the misanthropy of government bureaucracy–controlled solutions to social problems.)

In countries such as those mentioned above, it is or was not in the interest of those who rule to promote participation at the grass-roots level, because the primary government objective has been to control and to use the system to some specific power advantage. Yet, with the possible exception of Africa—whose meteorological, technological, and ethnological problems may continue to plague its political evolution well into the twenty-first century—the trend seems to be for more democracy and less autocracy throughout the world. And that desire for democracy extends from the Soviet block to China to Asia and most of Latin America. If ever there was a time to promote and develop a participative approach to world development, this is the time.

Yet, one discouraging setback in initiating a participatory development movement is the state of democracy in the United States. There is even some question as to whether it has the resolve to be an effective leader in developing and promoting a participative world development. However, like it or not—confused and frustrating as its political process is and will continue to be—the United States will nevertheless most likely be the country that leads the way, even if it is not capable of carrying out a sustained follow-through.

Chapter 1 of this book warned of the nondemocratic traditions that increasingly dominate the behavior of organizations and people in the United States. Ironically the country that created rule by the people is increasingly ruled not by the people, and the people are increasingly manipulated to believe that they still rule. We may automatically think of the United States as a leader in creating a world development (extending from its national myth of being a Christian nation that believes in the equality of all people). But the political reality of nonparticipation, if not checked, will permeate and distort our ability to effect any significant leadership.

Noam Chomsky, in particular, says that the manipulation of

the political process is having a corrosive effect on our democratic institutions.[1] Chomsky speaks of a wall going up between the political party intellectuals and the common citizens. People are no longer able to participate in the political process other than in what he calls a "ratification democracy," choosing between two candidates who have been selected by the parties with no interaction on the part of the people. (In the case of vice-presidents, even the ratification process is eliminated since the presidential candidate, alone, picks his vice-presidential candidate.)

In other words, there is no grass-roots mechanism by which you and I can play a real role or impart our views directly into the selection of those candidates who will ultimately be ratified by us. The party honchos do that. No doubt this is part of the reason for the indifference and apathy that the general population has toward the election process. Research reported in the organization-theory literature consistently verifies that, if people are not allowed to become intimately involved in the decision-making processes of an organization (and a country is an organization), they become apathetic toward it.

Is it totally cynical to think that this has come about by design? Again Chomsky feels that the "democratic" approach to government in the United States means having smart guys in the administration take charge and control the process specifically to eliminate the participation of the common person. He also feels that this is nothing new (albeit more sophisticated these days), for even the founding fathers were leery of involvement on the part of the undisciplined masses. The behavioral understanding of the apathy that comes from lack of participation, and the commitment that comes from involvement—so intensively researched and discussed in the past two decades—has always been intuitively understood by the leaders of humanity, and has been used for evil or good depending on their particular inclinations. One thinks of Hitler and his use of the grass-roots participation of the nation's thugs to implement his misanthropic view of global domination as a definite example of evil, and Christ's use of grass-roots participation by his disciples and converts and their converts after his death in the early centuries of Christianity (before the Romans legitimized and bureaucratized

it into the hierarchical and autocratic religious system it is now)—
spreading the message of love—as a clear example of good.

What can we do to change the political environment? Noam
Chomsky has some ideas on the subject, and so do I. Chomsky
recognizes that it is difficult for ordinary people, but that a primary way of becoming involved is to join in groups of shared
concerns, and discover together which directions to go.[2] Certainly a current international example of this is the Solidarity
movement in Poland, which began as a small group and has
expanded to a large national union whose members are constantly evaluating where they are and where they need to go.
And in September 1989, Solidarity was legitimized by the Polish
state, amid jubilant announcements to the world that democracy
had finally come to Poland.

Chomsky suggests that we need a proliferation of voluntary
organizations to replace the control and domination of the political parties. In voluntary organizations, hierarchical position
and bureaucratic domination—the bases of ownership and
power—are controlled by the people who make up the organization instead of by hierachically placed professionals. Cicela
Bok, too, says that volunteer groups have an advantage over
professional organizations: They eliminate the secrecy and lies
typical of present-day governments by putting the objectives
and operations of the organization out in the open.[3] Like Chomsky, Bok believes that small groups can lead to the development
of participative large-scale political organizations, which in the
end will make this country truly democratic.

This is all very powerful stuff, and addresses an all too unfortunate truth. One need only consult the participative management literature—which emphasizes the destruction of
hierachy and the role of the small group in promoting understanding, eliminating secrecy, developing commitment, and integrating all the people of an organization (and a nation is a big
organization)—to realize that, despite the polemics, Chomsky
is basically accurate in asserting that the reality of our democracy
does not match the myths.

Interestingly, the development of a volunteer approach to
world development could make a truly democratic country out
of the United States yet. That is, as volunteer networks are

developed to support projects in an integrated world development, they could in turn lead to a control of the political system in the United States through participative grass-roots organizations based on the small group. In any case, before we as a people go talking about the totalitarian behavior of other societies, we had better take another look at our own. There is much room for improvement.

Still I am optimistic that, in spite of the limitations of U.S. democracy, there is sufficient grass-roots organization to begin a world-development movement here. At this time in history—and despite the failings of our political process—there are enough Americans committed to change and a global development to get the ball rolling. And with luck, we may even help ourselves create a more democratic society in the United States.

To operate successfully in the long run, therefore, the volunteer development organization must hold a participative managerial philosophy. And given such a philosophical base, all members must be provided the opportunity to participate equally in the design and decision making required to operate the organization. There is no room for rank or hierarchy of members. Regardless of who they are—corporate executive, or janitor—in their professional lives, all are equal in the cooperative volunteer effort.

There is a rich and mostly ignored literature on the subject of participative managerial systems. That is, it has been mostly ignored by U.S. corporations, even though almost all of the techniques based on that philosophy were originally developed in the United States.

To illustrate how such a philosophy can motivate people, the example of one Japanese corporation—Mazda—using participation management to get the best from its employees will be presented in the next two sections. That will be followed by suggestions adapted from my earlier writings, on specific procedures for developing and maintaining effective volunteer work groups.

## THE INDUSTRIAL EXAMPLE

Participation is such an important ingredient to change and development because it springs from an essential human quality.

We are basically gregarious and are predisposed to cooperate with each other. In any change—technical or psychological—that will have a profound effect on a person, that person characteristically wants to be involved. This quality can be mobilized for a rapid and effective world development. If we would make dramatic changes in global society, those affected will have to give all they've got to make that change effective. They must participate in the process.

The Japanese have been the most effective in utilizing this very human quality in the past decade, for—at least in the 30% of Japanese industry (the giants such as Toyota) that we hear most about—participation has been the cornerstone of their success. One specific case is Mazda, which found itself in the mid–1970s with a major crisis: immanent bankruptcy. Its gas-guzzling, Wankel-powered ("rotary engine") cars would not sell in the pinch of the Arab oil embargo.[4] Already participative in its basic management orientation, the company went even further by involving blue-collar workers in its total operation. Production workers, for example, were converted into sales personnel during this period, in hopes of working off the inventory that had accumulated. After a year of this, it was found that the production-worker salespeople were greatly outselling the regular sales department. They had a better understanding of the car and what it could do, and they could thoroughly explain this to potential buyers.

Even more significantly, as things stabilized and the production workers returned to their regular jobs, they began suggesting changes that would both speed assembly and produce a better product. With the cooperation of management, this led to the formation of quality circles—small discussion groups where rank and authority are thrown out, as team members discuss how management and operations can be modified to maximize productivity. Thus, all its employees became involved in the management of Mazda. Its democratization went so far that the administrators started doing tours of duty as assembly-line workers, and the workers did stints as administrators, so that each group could better understand each other. The final outcome has been a blurring of the distinction between worker and administrator, as each group has participated and functioned in the same capacity as the other.

Incidentally, during this same period of time, Chrysler was also on the verge of bankruptcy. Chrysler maintained its white-collar forces and its social differentiation, sold facilities and land, and laid off a substantial number of blue-collar employees who have never been rehired. At Mazda, the salaries of all white-collar workers were reduced, but it did not lay off or reduce the salaries of its blue-collar labor force. Thus we have two different cultural views regarding the expediency of labor.

What Mazda is now doing with assembly-line workers is what we do with graduate engineers. Jobs such as the simultaneous handling of ten industrial robots (including the programming, maintenance, and scheduling of their operation) are routinely handled by workers on the floor. These are jobs that few U.S. companies would give to its blue-collar labor (and rightly so—given the education, training, and attitude of the average U.S. worker). Our industrial culture relies on an autocratic, adversarial distinction between labor and management that hasn't allowed participation or trust to develop.

## THE YO-YO ORGANIZATIONAL STRUCTURE

In a participatory organizational structure such as Mazda's, the hierarchical order is characteristically blurry—not unlike that of a truly volunteer organization, where participation and role reversals are an institutional way of life. The levels in a "yo-yo" organization constantly move up and down as a means of securing the commitment and creativity of each participant, and in the process all organizational members get an intimate understanding of the total operation.

At Mazda, workers and managers switch places periodically so that each will have a better understanding of what the other is thinking, how each fits within the organization, and what that means for improving organizational effectiveness. This may explain why Japanese managers invite blue-collar workers to their homes for dinner. They don't see that much difference between each other. It also helps explain why salary levels between lower level managers and workers is not nearly so profound as one finds in the United States.

As this up-and-down flow is the key ingredient of the Mazda environment, it is also the essential motivator of an effective volunteer organization. Hierarchy has no place in volunteerism. To be effective, a volunteer organization must be the epitome of participation. Otherwise, its organizational structure cannot be expected to survive in the long run, especially if coercion sets in. The effect of autocratic authority on unwilling subordinates can barely be sustained even in an environment where penalties such as termination and blacklisting are enforceable. In an environment where such threats have little chance of being enforced, such an operational philosophy has no chance whatsoever of being successful. Power has no place in the context of volunteerism, for people volunteer not to be controlled by others, but to serve a cause without conditions or controls imposed on how they offer their service.

Consequently, participation is the critical element in any serious effort to produce an effective, volunteer-driven world development. But there is much more to participative management than the Mazda example can demonstrate. The rest of this chapter will explain the specific dynamics associated with participation and volunteerism.

## PARTICIPATIVE MANAGEMENT AND JOINT DECISION MAKING

Although they were first presented thirty years ago, Warren Bennis's views on managerial approaches under complex organizational conditions are still valid.[5] Whenever one relies on the commitment of volunteers—and where it is not plausible to use brute force or the rigid rules of conduct that characterize bureaucracy (where Campbell's "unformed men" live within an imposed system that does not have to meet employee needs[6])—one must implement a very flexible and open style of management. Bennis identified the basic requirements as the following:

1. full and free communication, regardless of rank and power;
2. a reliance on consensus—rather than on the more customary forms of coercion—to manage conflict; and

3. a basically human bias that accepts both the inevitability of conflict in human interactions as well as the belief that group members can cope with and resolve that conflict.[7]

In an effective volunteer organization, full and free communication is absolutely essential—not regardless of rank and power, but because there is no rank and power as one would find in a bureaucratically controlled structure (which is typical of international development organizations). The ability of members to work together (particularly since there are no punishments to be feared) would rapidly break down under conditions of rank distinction between members. In fact, this is a far too common factor in the breakup of volunteer organizations, as anyone who has worked in them knows. (Consider what happens when a member of the local PTA goes "power mad.")

And since volunteer organizations rely so much on the use of small groups as the basis for getting things done, the only really effective means of managing is through the consensus process. This doesn't mean that everybody has to participate fully in every decision. In any volunteer effort, there are many times when a certain issue will not be relevant enough to some members, and those members will then decline to participate in that particular decision-making event. But it does mean that the opportunity to fully participate in consensus decision-making must always be available and that to aid that process, communication between members must always be free of rank and power.

Now we all know what a pain the consensus decision-making process can be. Yes, it is time consuming. And everyone must get to speak her or his peace before the group can come to any decision acceptable to all. But in the context of volunteer service, not allowing individuals to voice their concerns only assures that unresolved issues will turn into conflict further down the road. The time-consuming nature of consensus is precisely why most U.S. corporate institutions do not utilize it in their decision making. Also there is an explicit assumption among U.S. corporations that only managers have the knowledge and ability to make a rational decision. Workers are just too stupid. But in Japan, management approaches utilize consensus decision-making at all levels, and with outstanding success. This shows just how effective consensus can be even in the corporate world. And how much more so for volunteer organizations, then, is consensus—rather than coercion—essential to survival in small-group behavior, and to the use of small-group work teams in solving problems!

My whipping boy for the improper use of coercion on volunteers is again the Peace Corps, where decisions—as in corporate America—are made by managers (the representatives and directors of the field operations). The conflict and resentment generated by this situation has been a shared experience of virtually all volunteers. In the 1960s, disagreement with Peace Corps policy even resulted in dismissal; and for male volunteers, that in some cases translated into a death sentence. Two of my friends who were dismissed for disagreeing with policy (and in those days, you had to get money quickly—before your visa was cancelled—to fly out of the country, because the Corps would not pay your way back) found themselves immediately drafted, and were dead within six months. They had been placed in front-line battle units. (It was a commonly held belief that the Army's knowing you had been in the Peace Corps assured your being sent to a battle unit in Vietnam.) One learned to keep one's mouth shut during the Peace Corps tour, but the departure "parties" at the end were really quite dramatic. They consisted largely of pinning down one's administrators and yelling at the top of one's voice what absolute filth they were.

Nowadays—thanks to certain moderating acts of Congress— volunteers can exercise some right to dissent, and also have their return flights paid if they quit early or are dismissed. In fact, the Peace Corps organization is now paying for its past sins, for it has become almost fashionable among certain young people to sign on, do their duty for five or six months, and then quit in time to enter graduate school at the beginning of a semester. Given the past excesses of its management, I can't really bring myself to feel too sorry for the Corps. However, such behavior does raise holy hell in terms of maintaining the organization's staff and commitment to the country served. Once again, the message is that customary forms of coercive management do not work over the long run in a volunteer organization. To really commit themselves, people have got to be free, and must participate in the total operation of the organization.

Bennis also calls for consensus rather than coercion to manage conflict. Quite simply, in a volunteer organization, coercion can never work for the volunteer has nothing to lose when she or he is working "for nothing" to begin with. The idea of consensus rather than compromise is especially important to the volunteer organization because of the simple fact that volunteer activities are most often done in a small-group context.

In a larger and more formal setting, compromise may work better, because there is some distance between people and because the mechanics of getting large numbers of people to come to a consensus decision is extremely difficult. But in the setting of a small group (five to ten people), a compromise solution on an issue of conflict will ultimately kill the cooperation. In a for-profit organization, it will still kill the cooperation on the job; but, at least in the short run, things can be held together by coercion. Even then, there are ways that dissatisfaction can be expressed. My favorite example of this is from my student days, when I working an internship in a chemical plant. A particularly obnoxious industrial engineer publicly berated (one of his many sins) one of our co-workers. The "beratee" was not pleased. About two weeks later, the industrial engineer happened to be walking under a scaffold when a large valve accidentally fell on his head (which was covered by a safety helmet, although some of us wished that it hadn't been). He knew, and we knew, how the accident occurred. From that day on, he was a changed man—not through enlightenment, but from fear. Anonymous notes were sent to him; truck brakes "failed" when he was crossing the road, and so on. Eventually he was fired for incompetence: Quite simply, the man was too afraid to do his job anymore.

In the volunteer small group, you can't afford to let things get to the point where valves are being dropped (but, of course, we know that in some volunteer groups this does indeed happen). If a volunteer group can't resolve its conflicts on a consensus basis—which means that everybody, not just the majority, must be satisfied with its resolutions—then at some point in the future, the unsatisfied members will get their revenge. In a work environment where there are no formal coercive controls, such behavior will destroy the ability of the group to continue to work together. So how do you go about forming effective work groups?

Probably the best description is Douglas McGregor's eleven characteristics that distinguish an effective group from a not so effective one.[8] The first five descriptions include a theme that keeps coming up in this book, too: a lot of discussion, and participation by everybody. That participation is promoted by a comfortable working atmosphere. Above all, the effective group's objectives are well understood and accepted by all its members, and the classification and comprehension of those objectives come about because members listen to each other. There is disagreement, but the good group does not resort to the intimidation and tyrannical tricks that really destructive people use. When "there are disagreements which cannot be resolved," the group finds a way to deal with that.

The emphasis on participation is also critically important to the decision-making process of an effective volunteer group. As McGregor says, "Most decisions are reached by a kind of consensus in which it is clear that everybody is in general agreement and willing to go along. However, there is little tendency for individuals who oppose the action to keep their opposition private, and thus let an apparent consensus mask real disagreement." If a volunteer group does not have this open quality of decision making, it will pay at some future date when a repressed member decides to get even.

And finally, the leader of the effective small group has something of the nature of Lao-tzu: She or he does not dominate or behave in an autocratic matter. This is absolutely essential in a volunteer arrangement; members rightly feel that they are not in a subordinate relationship. And in fact, as McGregor notes, "different members, because of their knowledge or experience, are in a position to act as resources of the group. The members utilize them in this fashion, and they occupy leadership roles while they are thus being used." I would add that this switching of leadership roles is probably continuous in a volunteer group—

the leader being more of a facilitator and troubleshooter than a leader as ordinarily defined.

And that's all one really has to know to develop and facilitate a good working group. Of course, a poor working group has all the opposite attributes. And McGregor adds that, in a good group, people still remain individuals but their commitment to the common purpose allows their individuality to be sufficiently muted so as not to become destructive of the group purpose.

Returning, then, to Bennis's thoughts on management, he calls for a basically human bias that will encourage emotional expression and an acceptance of the inevitability of conflict in human interactions, coupled with the belief that members can cope with and mediate that conflict. This is the cornerstone of any effective volunteer effort. Volunteers working together for any decent length of time must utilize a managerial control that emphasizes constructive solutions to problems as they arise and engage in a continuous dialogue that is free from the intervention of rank or power. When those basic elements are not in play, volunteer efforts succumb to the same organizational failings that corporate organizations in the United States have so often ignominiously achieved. The beauty in developing small volunteer groups, however, is that there is a basic human propensity satisfied in the process (as explained in Chapter 1), enabling people to work together.

## GROUP PERFORMANCE ATTRIBUTES

The underlying managerial philosophy of a volunteer organization, as well as the management and function of working groups within that organization, must be inherently participative. And when I say participative, I mean it in the fullest sense. There can be no separation of members by rank or power (unless members voluntarily and on a consensus basis decide that is necessary).

To be committed for the long term and to give their all, volunteers must be allowed to be participants in all managerial processes. That, of course, doesn't mean that they should be compelled to participate, but the opportunity to do so must always be available. In regard to those who are reluctant to take part in decision-making activities, I recall one of my experiences in training South American government officials to use participative management approaches. This was a particularly tough bunch of autocratic cookies, and it was necessary for me to get pretty demanding as I ran them through an assortment of learning exercises. After three days of this, a Brazilian (who had been particularly autocratic at the beginning of the session) demanded and got time to complain to the whole work group that, in trying to make them participative in outlook, I was being more autocratic than they were. I acknowledged his point, and told them that their governments had given me the power of God to control and direct them through a week of hell. I made no apologies. Well, a good volunteer who just really doesn't want to get into decision making shouldn't be forced to. My management trainees, on the other hand—in the unique circumstances of the organizational development environment—had no choice.

Frank Cassell has summarized well the orientation of the administrator in a traditional organization, who on the basis of hierarchy makes important decisions affecting subordinates and co-workers.

The conventional business stand is in favor of strong top-down government as against grass roots neighborhood decision-making because the former is perceived as the most efficient way to govern. . . . The businessman is a top-down person. That is how he is selected, how he is trained, and how he is developed in an environment which is essentially authoritarian and carefully structured. Important decision-making is limited to the few at the top; and those at the bottom are expected to comply. In some magical way hierarchical position seems to confer wisdom regardless of knowledge or experience; those down the line with less status have less wisdom and competence.[9]

And that is exactly what one cannot have in a volunteer organization: hierarchical inferiors. A healthy volunteer organization must avoid such a managerial structure because it will only add to the conflicts that arise. People guilty of hierarchical behavior are not good at controlling conflict anyway. The setup that Cassell describes will greatly tax the effectiveness of a volunteer group's activity.

Given, then, that the volunteer organization has developed its work groups adequately enough to control conflict and promote participation, what are some of the attributes of small groups that enable volunteers to work together effectively?

Likert long ago defined the performance characteristics of a good working group; and among those characteristics, the following remain important to the proper functioning of a volunteer work group:

• A group should be in existence long enough to establish a relaxed working relationship among all its members (and that, to a large extent, will be determined by its ability to monitor and control conflicts as they develop among group members).

• Members need to help each other be satisfied with what they do in the group. In fact, creating an atmosphere in which members feel they can do the impossible will further fine-tune the group's overall working effectiveness.

• The development and maintenance of a supportive atmosphere by specifically avoiding rank-and-power managerial controls (as described earlier in the chapter) further stimulates creativity.

• And above all, an effective group understands the value of "constructive conformity." That is, many times there are routine decisions that don't need a consensus resolution; they aren't that important to the group's functioning. It is then helpful to have a conformity that will eliminate the waste of time on fruitless discussion.[10]

While performance characteristics such as these may be difficult to attain in an adversarial work environment (such as in U.S. corporations), good volunteer groups are in a much better position to function within these guidelines because by definition they do not have the coercive elements.

## A SUMMATION OF PARTICIPATIVE VOLUNTEER STRUCTURES

Finally, the personal satisfactions that come from working with a volunteer group are enjoyable to the participants themselves and also help maintain the group's long-term survival. In a very real sense, members receive as much as they give. Peace

Corps trainers look for the volunteer who expresses a balanced motivation toward volunteering. Potential volunteers who talk most of the time about saving malnourished babies or—on the other hand—relaxing on a beach for two years just won't cut it. But when they talk about helping others as well as gaining some knowledge of the world and a little adventure, then trainers' ears pick up because there may be something to work with.

Thus, a good volunteer group member directly benefits from very specific personal need satisfactions, and these need satisfactions come under the paradigm that Abraham Maslow made popular in the 1950s. The reward that one gets from working in a group is something I have described earlier in *Organization for Rural Development*.[11] I shall repeat here a particularly relevant passage.

Following the individual-need-satisfaction approach of Maslow's need-satisfaction hierarchy, group members can also satisfy physical, social, egoistic, and self-actualization needs through the group. For example, group members can satisfy physical needs through the group (if they were in a corporation such as Mazda) by immersing themselves in group activities, which as a result of the group's success can lead to the direct payment of food or money to each individual member or a future payment that satisfies physical needs. In the process, members who are part of a tight, cohesive group know that they have other members to lean on for physical and moral support or help in making a major decision that can affect the quality of their livelihood. Certainly, group interaction fulfills an individual's social need (Maslow's second stage) the need for affiliation with other humans. A basic condition of all human cultures is a need of most individuals of that culture to belong to and be a part of a group. Most people want to interact with other people and fortunately for most of us, we have not yet been reduced, despite the onslaught of our increasingly anomic society, to that of the Ik, a West African tribe that was removed from its former hunting grounds and in the process of that transfer and cultural degradation developed a truly bestial (that went lower than the beasts) society of the survival of the fittest. The Ik found that love or concern for another had no place in the new society. Consequently, new survival mechanisms developed whereby adult children had no compunction about abandoning starving parents and in fact would even steal food from them. Mothers would casually discard newborns (a behavior which even Tasmanian Devil mothers do not exhibit) and so forth. Unfortunately, in the evolving character of the American underclass, one can see similar patterns developing as did among the Ik. But under less overwhelming pathos, most people do want to interact and help others. This basic reality of the human condition, the need to care for each other, when applied to the development of effective volunteer groups, is one that can be effectively exploited to the benefit of a world development.

Arguments for satisfaction of other needs may also be made. For example, some groups may allow certain individuals to perceive themselves as having more prestige and consequently more ego satisfaction by being a member of a successful group. Whether that is a precondition for joining a group or the consequence of participating in a successful group, it is definitely a need that can be satisfied. Even self-actualization needs can be satisfied through group functions. Individuals who can show other group members how to perform a job better or lead the group to better accomplishments, it can be argued, are experiencing self-actualization as much as an artist or writer is. Within the confines of the group membership those people are engaging in new, creative, skillful activities that satisfy the individual, and are respected by other group members. Again, whether or not this is a precondition for or consequence of effective group interaction, like the quest for ego satisfaction, such individual needs can be satisfied through the group and thereby further reinforce the cohesiveness and ability of a group to function together on a long-term basis.[12]

Thus, a healthy group member is concerned about personal satisfaction. If a volunteer is happy with the workings of the group, then she or he will most likely stay with it. While I'm sure a specialist in small-group dynamics would give a more detailed explanation of the psychology of the individual group member, it really boils down to personal satisfaction and the reward feelings that come from working with the group as well as providing service to the target clients. Power, rank, and a lack of opportunity to participate in decision making will only impede the effectiveness of a volunteer work group. Personal satisfaction is important to the long-term survival of any volunteer organization.

## WHAT ABOUT THE RECIPIENT COUNTRIES?

We must also be concerned with the actions and behavior of officials in the recipient countries that the volunteer development groups will serve. What are their views on participation and interaction? As presented in Chapter 2, the bureaucracy picture is not all that pleasant. In some places, the development group (the work group with village counterparts) may wind up being viewed as a threat to the power of government officials. In fact, this is bound to happen in certain countries. And when it does, there is little that can then be done to aid the country through volunteer mechanisms.

But even that scenario does not have to be accepted as the inevitable final outcome. There are ways by which individual linkages and whole agencies within the host governments can become more cooperative and participative in their interaction with a volunteer world development. And that is by utilizing the techniques of organizational change—more specifically, an organizational change that promotes participation. I have written extensively about that host-country change process, and will cite from my own *Organizational Change and the Third World*.[13] in the following section. It is possible—albeit somewhat difficult— to "create" host-country bureaucratic counterparts who are receptive to the participative group process, and who can work effectively with volunteer development groups.

## CHANGING THE ORGANIZATIONAL PEOPLE

Not surprisingly, the effective initiation of organizational change depends upon the kind and quality of people responsible for the changes made within the home organization. The origin of the initiation of the process can be both internal and external. Focusing on the external first, there are two common ways to initiate organizational change. One way is indirect, through international educational programs (be they Marxist or Capitalist inspired). Certainly this writer has trained enough Latin American, Iranian, and African students to hope that all the training they got on participation, group decision-making, and organization development will be applied once they return to their homelands. Consequently, this indirect external approach could become an internal force as administrators within their organizations try a more democratic method after coming to power. The logic is that my students and other similarly trained students will be there to help, but given that early middle age is the power years, in most cases that would occur 30 years from now.

One of the strategies that has received the most professional attention in the past several years is the external training of people from developing countries in out-of-country, short-term programs on management techniques. While such efforts may not focus fully on organizational change, they certainly introduce some of the elements of organizational change that under the right leadership could be a positive force for change within the host-country institutions that those people return too.

The reader may not be aware of some of the simplest management skills that many of these external training courses provide. For example, in such training programs there are people who have never thought of defining objectives before planning a project, and who have never considered using a relatively simple evaluation process such as a matrix evaluation—let alone using groups as a vehicle for group decision making. Few such people, on their own, would consider including in the planning process the participation of the people to be affected by a new program.

This, however, is not meant to be all that critical for I recently had the same experience while consulting for a large local organization involved in a long-term planning project. I found that managers viewed specifying one's objectives, criteria, and project evaluation technique as somewhat of a revelation (let alone the idea of letting company grunts participate in the decision-making process within the organization). So the reluctance to change is not restricted to the third world. But there are more direct ways to try to get a change in the behavior of the people volunteer groups will have to work with.

And I must break off there, on a provocative note. I suggest that interested readers consult the cited work to gain a more comprehensive understanding of the process of changing organizations.

## PROSPECTS FOR THE FUTURE

Well, for twenty years I've been teaching, consulting, and writing on this subject of changing the behavior of host-country officials; and the record is mixed, to say the least. There have been outstanding successes, and a lot of failures. Still I'm optimistic that we may be finally reaching the takeoff point. People trained in the early years are now reaching positions in their organizations where they can behave in the manner they accepted in their training. And the effect of the Soviets suddenly packing in and urging participation cannot be overlooked. Combine all this with the less threatening profile of volunteer groups working with counterparts in the villages, and we may just be able to pull it off, entering a new age of development work. One thing is certain: It will be an age in which people directly help other people, eliminating the dysfunctional bureaucratic interventions that have proved for the most part ineffective over the past twenty years.

There will continue to be obstacles, and there will need to be a change in the way certain countries officials interact with the volunteers of world development. Simply, the officials will have to accept (just as the Soviets have) that, if effective development is to occur in their countries, it will require a participative interaction between them, the citizens they control, and the volunteer development groups that they all work with. Of course, this will mean the loss of some power on the part of those who have it, but better the loss of some power than the higher price in the end when socioeconomic troubles spiral a society into anarchy. The Soviet Union has given the entire world a gift in daring to make its recent changes. It has shown that autocracy and oppression do not work in the development of a modern society. Among those Third World countries that haven't already tried the Soviet model of development, there is now no need to, for its inadequacies have been clearly demonstrated.

We must change the behavior of those autocratic officials and bureaucrats whom I have so consistently criticized throughout this book. It is possible to change a sincere manager-type person through organizational development training. While she or he may never be a total convert to participation and freedom, that person can at least become a reasonably effective administrator who will not impede or harm the interactive process that should go on in development between the people helped and those who help them.

So in the end we will need a global organizational structure that can merge the three old socioeconomic worlds as we map a pathway to a brand new world development. The First World will recognize and establish participative volunteer networks as the primary vehicle for creating a global development movement, supported—but not controlled—by national development agencies. Officials in the Third World will (hopefully quickly) change their operational philosophies to an acceptance of participation and equality of power in relationships between volunteer development groups and the people those groups help.

In the process, something will evolve—as yet unknown—that will help to create a new egalitarian and truly global society. Perhaps even our grandchildren (with an enculturated concern for an egalitarian and global society; see Chapter 7) will inherit this more peaceful and fruitful Earth. And the cornerstone of that bright future—very simply—is an acceptance that participation and involvement by all actors in the management of human lives and development is first in the global bill of rights that will lead us into an even greater 10,000 forthcoming years of civilization.

Participation and shared control fit the human condition so well. They served us in our small-group bands of Homo erectus and early Homo sapiens, before we lost these basic tools of social behavior in the process of becoming civilized. The heavy baggage of control inherited from the early days of civilization is largely still with us. But we are beginning to shed it; and moreover, we now have the technology to shed it. Things are looking up.

## SUMMARY

One of the primary concerns of this chapter has been to show that participation, joint decision making, and the use of small groups are all key to the long-term success of volunteer organizations and their linkage with host countries. As well as giving to others, the volunteer also receives, in terms of experience and the rewarding state of mind she or he achieves. This may not necessarily be a religious experience, but it's pretty close to that. I am reminded of the biblical parable that tells of a master who sends his servant to get the best and worst pieces of meat. The servant brings back two tongues and explains that there is nothing so bad as a bad tongue and nothing so good as a good tongue. The same goes for working in small volunteer groups. There is nothing so good as working with a good small group, and nothing so bad as working with a bad small group. We'll need plenty of the good ones to sustain a volunteer world-development movement.

And to prevent potential badness from developing, every volunteer organization must remain vigilant with regard to its small-group dynamics. It will need to monitor the overall healthiness of its membership all the time, to make sure that interpersonal events do not become destructive and damage the effectiveness of the organization. Fortunately, the shared motivation of all members to work for the same goals and objectives without the interference of rank and salary does automatically improve the dynamics. People who want power and can't have it will more than likely not be joining a participative development group in the first place. But nevertheless, we must remain watchful of the little things that can complicate and make dysfunctional a good group's efforts. Ultimately, even participative volunteer groups need to incorporate certain organizational elements, and that is the subject of Chapter 5.

## NOTES

1. Noam Chomsky interview on *A Conversation with Bill Moyers*, PBS Television, September 20, 1988.

2. Ibid.

3. Cicela Bok interview on *A Conversation with Bill Moyers*, PBS Television, October 6, 1988.

4. *Manufacturing Miracles*, PBS Television, November 10, 1988.

5. Warren Bennis, *Changing Organizations* (New York: McGraw-Hill, 1960). p. 573.

6. Joseph Campbell, *The Power of Myth* (New York: Doubleday, 1988), p. 145.

7. Bennis, *Changing*. p. 573.

8. D. McGregor, *The Human Side of Enterprise* (New York: McGraw-Hill, 1960), p. 233.

9. Frank Cassell, "The Corporation and Community Realities and Myths," in *Fundamentals of Management; Selected Readings*, ed. James Donnelly, Jr. (Dallas: Business Publications, 1975), p. 358.

10. Rensis Likert, "The Nature of Highly Effective Groups," in *Readings on Behavior in Organizations*, ed. Edgar Huse, James Bowditch, and Dalmor Fisher. (New York; Addison-Wesley, 1975), p. 139.

11. A. Jedlicka, *Organizational for Rural Development* (New York: Praeger, 1977).

12. Ibid. p. 62.

13. A. Jedlicka, *Organizational Change and the Third World* (New York: Praeger, 1987).

# FIVE

# Some Elements of
# Organization Relevant to a
# World Development

As we approach the twenty-first century, it becomes ever more
certain that the organizational means by which our economic
systems function and by which our national systems interact
with each other will have to change. Particularly so as we try to
integrate more closely and produce a world development that
distributes the economic pie equitably among all countries. Fortunately, much of the organizational change theory needed to
create that new organizational form already exists.

Long ago, we human beings learned that the hierarchical,
bureaucratic model of organization outlined in Chapter 2 can
survive and even be effective in the short run. The classic example of this is the military, where rigid obedience to the battle-
condition hierarchy can reduce the loss of lives as well as win
battles. But in the long run, such rigid obedience can limit the
total effectiveness of the unit. The Israelis, with their citizen
army, have long recognized such short-run limitations and consequently operate on a two-tier system.[1] During a battle, the
Israeli fighting units rely on a rigid command bureaucracy; but
before the battle, all soldiers participate in deciding how they
will fight, within the sphere of their unit. They revert to command authority only when the battle takes place. In more relaxed
periods between wars, the fighting units dissolve, and soldiers
return to their civilian occupations until again called into action.

The oppression of the command bureaucracy never has a chance to affect the creativity and participative decision-making of unit members, because its existence is so short-term. This provides the units with the best of both worlds: the initiative and creativity of civilian life, combined with the high level of training, group decision-making, and motivation to win that come from a specialized military training.

The Israeli Army serves as an analogy for the organization of a volunteer-controlled world development. Certainly there are and always will be times when hierarchical command bureaucracy is necessary to carry out a particular task, but it must only be a tool that participative, nonauthoritarian, and self-actualizing organizations use in an emergency. And its use must be authorized voluntarily by the members. For long-term success, an effective organization must build and rely on the creativity and commitment of its team members, without coercion. This has in fact been a major failing of U.S. production organizations, which too often institutionalize command bureaucracy as their standard operating procedure rather than handling it as an emergency tool. And attributing workplace autocracy only to the floor managers' ignorance, laziness, or egoistic needs is highly suspect. In any case, this use of what should be an emergency tool as the modus operandi makes for alienated employees who will produce just exactly what they have to and no more. It does not produce the self-actualizing, aggressive, involved employee who can help the organization accomplish and sustain its central objectives. And it definitely won't work in volunteer organizations.

Furthermore, the bureaucratic models that international development agencies are so fond of (see Chapter 2 again) cannot produce the creativity and flexibility to deal with a challenging environment that a participative structure would. In short, more power and control must go to the lower levels of organizations, if a successful development process is to occur.

Thus—whether for the development of a more fair world, or for the maximization of profits, in the twenty-first century— eliminating the excesses of bureaucracy in all organizations now is paramount. That the United States is finally becoming aware of this necessity is fortunate. It may be too late, however, since countries such as Japan and Germany are already ahead of us in utilizing the creative potential of participative decision-making. In the case of an integrated world-development effort that is not concerned with making a profit, and whose members will function to serve humanity, a rigid bureaucratic structure with strict adherence to autocratic control won't even get off the ground. The membership of these organizations will be professionals in volunteerism, and volunteers do not salute or genuflect. But even in the for-profit production organizations, Japan has clearly showed that nineteenth-century arrangements that recommend the brutalization of employees will no longer bring the results that an organization needs to survive in the modern world. (The story of how Mazda Corporation motivates its employees was provided in Chapter 4.)

Unquestionably, the direction of organizational change in the twenty-first century will be to a nonhierarchical participative mode where individuals can more closely match their personal goals with those of the organization. But in the twilight of the twentieth century (until most production is replaced by robotics), we will continue to see some reactionary uses of nineteenth-century management in the last few remaining smokestack, sweatshop industries. This is a very short term phenomenon. One problem will be the retraining of people to function in the new human resource–oriented industries—particularly in the United States, where workers will have to think just as much in the short term as their employers. Also, a human resource orientation assumes lots of individual responsibility. The U.S. educational system (as it now stands) has difficulty creating that kind of worker. One recent piece of depressing news is the National Personnel Management Society's projection that a growth area for graduates in the education field is the training of people who can effectively teach young workers who lack basic literacy and mathematical skills.

Again we see the short-term solution, especially in the service industries that presently face a labor shortage; on-the-job training programs that bring workers up to at least marginal proficiency, adequate enough to do the largely unskilled jobs they perform. Responding to that problem more generally—and in keeping with the more nurturing behavior that will be needed in the twenty-first century to foster world development—are the various volunteer tutor programs for illiterates that have cropped up all over the country. Television, through its public service announcements, has been good at informing the public of the extent of the problem. But unfortunately, such efforts don't really seem to be significantly affecting the problem. Literacy and education in general continue to go downhill. The implications for the immediate future of the United States—where workers must have a better understanding of math, science, and language to operate the new technologies—is not encouraging. A human resource retraining campaign on the part of the U.S. corporations could help temporarily as a band-aid approach, but a human resource focus also requires workers to be mature enough to assume the individual responsibility that will make them effective, productive workers. In the United States the educational system doesn't create enough of this kind of people.

The society that is best developing such people is Japan (which is now known and applauded for its use of management systems that both improve products and provide greater worker satisfaction). Many efforts have been made in the United States to duplicate the success of the Japanese; but, specifically in regard to the individual-responsibility factor, a major difference exists between the Japanese and the U.S. worker: the extent of education and training that the Japanese worker receives.

Every Japanese student, regardless of her or his final occupational destination, takes the same high school curriculum: a heavy dose of math, science, and foreign languages. The blue-collar worker then takes an additional four years of specialized training in the technology and production systems that she or he will be working with.[2] The educational process never stops. Job retraining is a constant fact of life among Japanese workers. What all this investment yields is a corps of highly skilled workers and managers who are well prepared to communicate with fellow workers and who are technically prepared to deal with the demands of a complex and ever-changing technology.

Notice that the Japanese worker is more than merely technically proficient. She or he is also interpersonally proficient, having skills that are highly relevant to the world-development scheme described here. This is partly a reflection of the Japanese culture, as well as being a specific policy of large Japanese corporations. The Japanese routinely rely on group dynamics and consensus making as a means of involving people in joint decision-making, both off the job and on it.

In the job environment of Japan, the primary tool of participation is the quality circle (actually invented by an American, John Deming). Small groups of workers, facilitated by a team leader, collectively discuss ways in which the productive processes that they are responsible for can be improved. Not only does such decision making (through the synergism of the group process) lead to highly profitable, precisely relevant changes in production processes, but it also leads to a higher state of worker commitment. Employees feel that they are part of a community, and they are indeed contributing directly to the industrial community to which they belong. (A discussion of how small groups function was provided in Chapter 4.)

The Japanese worker's American counterpart may all too often have a high school education but be barely able to write, let alone engage in group discussions on methods by which productivity can be increased. Yet it is exactly this ability to interface in the group context that will be vital both to the continued economic well-being of the developed countries, as well as to the smooth operation of an international network effecting world development. It will be necessary to utilize the strengths and motivational benefits of the good working group to do the job.

It's not that we haven't known about the need for effective group skills in this country—not only for industrial productivity, but also for better global understanding. As early as 1951 Samuel Everett wrote,

Children [need to] develop skills in group living through co-operation, determining group purposes, methods, and evaluation in the classroom. It is often lack of training in group thinking and group action that wrecks international conferences, and family relationships. Children can learn the art of compromise and of the development of consensus in and through their activities in elementary school.[3]

But it seems we never followed through in our educational systems (at least with any coordinated effort that would bear fruit). That doesn't mean, however, that we can't start now. Chapter

7 will examine what is presently going on in this area of child-hood education, as well as what can be done to improve group-dynamics training at the elementary level.

At the present time, the Japanese are certainly ahead of every-body else in the areas of group decision-making and participative organizations. Furthermore, there is the very real possibility that they will increase their effectiveness even more, through the use of advanced computers. I see that as helping to promote a world development in the long run, for we can expect the Japanese to continue advancing in the human group-machine interface that necessarily comes about when using state-of-the-art computers (specifically, fifth generation computers). In the short run, such advances will undoubtedly extend the lead that Japanese in-dustry already enjoys in the changing technology of industrial production. But in the long run, as I say, it will provide an experience-based knowledge that can be helpful in changing society and creating structures that promote a world develop-ment. We will return to this positive role of the computer later in the chapter.

In creating a volunteer-controlled world development, it would indeed be useful to have a pool of people with the group decision-making skills of the Japanese and the reputed creativity of the Americans. With such a combination, development teams would have access to the creativity of individual members and yet offer all the social advantages that a group provides in nur-turing, fine-tuning, and operationalizing good ideas. One thing is certain: World development through volunteerism will have to operate in a group context, for the ability of individuals alone (with a few notable exceptions) to carry out a sustained effort is limited. One needs the support of equally concerned and effec-tive team members.

Creative people can be trained to work effectively in the small group, and our educational process can do the job. In fact, to some extent, this has already been done. For example, long ago at Northwestern University, I trained engineering students in the remedial mathematics classes to work via small groups. The synergistic effect of working together greatly improved their grasp of mathematics individually. It wouldn't have taken a great deal more effort to turn those groups into training sessions for group project work in their future engineering careers. This was nothing particularly radical. In fact, it conformed with certain basic practices of the U.S. public school system, for in the elementary schools children are quite commonly taught in small groups. But somewhere in middle school and high school, the approach is dropped, and is replaced with the lecture format. The Japanese, on the other hand, continue using small-group formats throughout and even add a "one-room schoolhouse" dimension in that brighter students help slower students to learn the material.

All too often, getting Americans to work effectively in this participative group role can be difficult. A case in point is the organizational development course that I teach at present. Students are required to work for a complete semester on a field-based problem, and with a real client in a local enterprise who is having an organizational problem. Before entering my class, these students have had three years of university instruction on a strictly lecture basis, which has offered them very little interaction either on a group basis or within the lecture format. Suddenly they are in a situation where they have to initiate contact with a client, develop a research design that makes sense, defend their design, and develop solutions based on the conceptual information that they have been taught in previous courses and the real-time research that they do in their client organizations. This is a eye-opening experience for just about everybody; and while most finally adjust and are reasonably effective, about a third never do. They become a burden to the rest of the group members. Yes, the class can be quite traumatic, but its intent is to give students the opportunity to become competent initiators of change through the group process.

A group whose members understand each other can work together to produce results that are more than they could ever be through individual effort. This advantage of group work is directly relevant to the world-development effort, for such an effort will require the collaboration and shared commitment that only a good working group can provide. Consequently, the first step in developing an effective world-development organization is to recognize that team development will be its key operational element.

## INDIVIDUALS, GROUPS, AND COMPUTERS

A second element that will play a significant role in volunteer world-development organizations is the linkage between individuals, groups, and computer systems. The Japanese, again, are pushing for the integration of work teams and computer systems that comprehend the latest change processes. This is consistent with the cultural milieu of that country: "The Japanese are used to group decision-making and they see the Fifth Generation [computers] as a means of smoothing that consensual process."[4]

In fact, the fifth generation computer could turn out to be the enfant terrible of the next century. Its primary distinction over today's computers is that it will basically think as a human does yet still retain the binary computational advantages of a digital computer. In a sense, it will be something brighter and more rationally capable than humans.

The Japanese, as illustrated a few years ago in a MacNeil/Lehrer report, have a particularly un-American view of robots and computers. They regard them as—in more than one sense—equals, so that the fifth generation computers may very well (at least in the Japanese society) become team members and not just adjunct tools to the design and decision-making activities of the human work groups.[5]

In the MacNeil/Lehrer report, Japanese workers were shown exercising with the company robots during preshift calisthenics. Workers discussed their robots as if they were fellow human workers. Americans—on the other hand—regard robots as tools, not comrades. It is interesting to note that the only human ever killed by a robot (in violation of Asimov's first law of robotics) was an American in a Ford assembly plant.

In the strategic planning of Japanese governmental agencies such as the Ministry of International Trade (MITI) as well as our own NASA, the increasing view is evidently that

the best way to accomplish useful things is through connected effort by a large group, instead of the inspired work of one outstanding genius[.] The Apollo project to put man on the moon was not the work of a solitary genius, but a series of well-orchestrated efforts by many well-trained and knowledgeable people. The same is true of successful firms, governmental agencies, military adventures, and performing arts. Our myth of a glorious rugged individualism, whether in the log cabin or inside the human cranium, is dear to us, but is a fiction that doesn't stand up to inspection under twentieth-century circumstances.[6]

One could argue for individual creativity versus group synergism in the area of product development; but a fifth generation computer would still be in the picture, eliminating the drudgery of statistical computation and data searching that had to be done by one or more humans in the past. In fact, the fifth generation computer could be the bridge between creative individuals working alone and the resourceful work team, by eliminating the mechanical drudgery of research and development. In any case, the computer can release human energies to explore creative alternatives, whatever the endeavor.

In terms of producing a world development, fifth generation computers could make irrelevant the quest for ever greater international market control. Consumer production might become so cheap and so easy that it will eliminate the pecuniary motives that have so dominated industrial activities in past centuries. Finally, a major breakthrough in fusion technology would provide the cheap energy for such a world. Science fiction stories have long described such a futuristic cornucopia—and it will happen, too—but for a while yet, it is likely that at least some countries will still be stuck in a nineteenth-century concept of dominating world economic systems.

For example, some say that the Japanese are single-mindedly concerned with maintaining and capturing global markets to become the primary geo-economic power—thus conquering the world not through war (a strategy they tried in earlier years), but through the sheer force of their economic, team, and interactive computer skills.

If that be the case—well, obviously, this is not what we need for world development in the twenty-first century, no matter how advanced the technology and interactive skills. Removing the veneer of technology and behavioralism from such a scheme, it is not really all that different from mercantilism in the sixteenth century, when countries utilized their technological and organizational advantages to produce and sell products to the rest of the world—carefully retaining the profits, hiding the technology, and treating all other countries as kept markets to be exploited by the developers of the technology.

We should be able to expect more than this from all the developed countries in the twenty-first century. If the only thing countries such as the United States and Japan can do is to come up with ever more efficient ways of economic exploitation (and the United States is increasingly not good at it), then as a culture we can only expect (as well as deserve) more of what we are seeing at the end of the twentieth century: a politics of desperation in the non–First World. This manifests itself in such strategies as a barrage of terrorism, and an increasing ability to bankrupt the economic and banking systems of the First World via the debtors' cartel. But that theme doesn't have to keep playing; and as continued accommodation with the Soviet bloc emerges, so does the chance to create a world development using some of the money that disarmament will free up.

One thing is certain: Computers will play an increasingly important role throughout human society—in the economic production systems of the First World and the Third, as well as in eliminating the drudgery of routine coordination within and between volunteer development groups. (How this can be done will be explained in Chapter 6.)

Still, any effective organizational structure in the service of world development will still need a human interface. Even fifth generation computers cannot be expected to have the element of compassion that will probably always separate us from intelligent machines. And while it would be nice to create a mechanism for world development that is free of organizational levels and bureaucracy, the simple reality is that one cannot—at least not on a macro scale. By contrast, the micro-level organization can be rather fluid, as illustrated by the autonomous projects of some individual churches. While I am certainly not denigrating such efforts, the truth is that individual efforts are a drop in a vast bucket. We have to create a volunteer system that has the participative and member-control advantages of micro approaches and the impact of large-scale macro efforts. And on top of that, any sign of the institutional excesses so typical of bureaucracies must be curbed.

The fear, naturally, in creating volunteer organizational structures is that in the end they will become no better than the professional development agencies criticized in Chapter 2. However, there is a certain built-in control in that the philosophical base—people helping other people without monetary reward—will screen out those who are looking for economic or power advantages. A system of automatic rotation and grass-roots control of positions that have the possibility of being abused will further ensure that the volunteers focus on satisfying the human needs that provoked the development effort (see Chapter 4). And there are applicable organizational models that already exist—one of them being the time-tested role of the agricultural extension agent.

## THE EXTENSION AGENT AS ORGANIZATIONAL MODEL

Peter Drucker mentions the farm agent at the turn of the century as the key social innovator concerned with maximizing economic and productive systems in the United States.[7] The farm agent was actually a creation of Sears Roebuck and Company's Julius Rosenwald, who wanted his customers to improve their earnings so they could buy more Sears products. To a great extent, we can trace the success of our agriculture to the farm agent, in terms of both farm production as well as the dissemination of other ideas that led to improved economic performance. Capturing Rosenwald's organization theory for rapidly introducing technology, the Department of Agriculture (USDA) used the Sears system as a model in setting up its network of state and county extension offices. Similarly, the farm agent now serves as a key to Third World agricultural programs (although support and training is still too often deficient).[8]

Extension is an important element of any kind of grass-roots work, be it in the developed or developing countries. In the United States, for example, there is an extension effort currently involved in getting teenagers to understand the threat of AIDS and the importance of using condoms (a formerly taboo subject that one now finds even in the story plot of television sitcoms). Residents of low-income housing are often organized into voting blocks by political extension agents, and—yes—even farmers are being reorganized into a modern version of the old Grange movement in an effort to retake control of the politico-economic forces that harass them at this point in history.

Common to all of these movements is the extension structure with its agents, who must have the behavorial skills to motivate and instruct recipients in the acceptance and use of alternatives. I have described these attributes elsewhere and will summarize them here by excerpting from that work.

There is some question as to whether most countries recognize the importance of an effective extension network, and the role agents play in it. While some developing countries are often eager to adopt and emulate the technological development styles of the United States and other developed countries, they often overlook the significance of the role the extension agent has played and still plays in the transfer of technologies to farmers, industrialists, and other professional and non-professional organizations in the developing countries. He may be called something else, such as a liaison coordinator, or communication-interface specialist, but basically he is an extension agent in every sense of the word. Because developing-country change institutions do not recognize the importance of this transfer function, extension jobs often are low-paid, nonprestigious, overworked occupations performed by ill-trained, poorly motivated people who therefore virtually insure the failure of any effort to transfer technology.

The only way to correct the situation is through an investment of time and funds in the development of training programs that can pro-duce the kind of agent who will do the job well. The fact is that programs developing these people are not cheap, but there are some cost advan-tages in that these people can effectively service a larger number of technology recipients (when properly supported) through such transfer approaches [than] the use of trained work groups as the unit of transfer.[9]

But if extension agents are to be effective, they must be spe-cially trained so as to carry out the joint role of facilitator and participant.

Extension agents can either present information to the transfer group and interact in the group processes along with the elected leader-representative of the group, or act as the sole linking agent in cases where there is specialized and complex information from the upper levels of the organization to be transmitted to group members. That calls for a whole host of traits . . . which can benefit the extension agent in his efforts; among these are empathy, homophyly, and credibility (determined in part by client perceptions of his institutional connection).

For example, the likelihood of having an empathetic extension agent can be increased by selecting people who come from the client's cultural background and consequently are well acquainted with the client's problems. It sometimes can be gained by requiring the uninitiated agent to live in the client's environment for a time during the agent's training (a common practice in the Peace Corps). Homophylous change agents, who may or may not be empathetic (some people reject their former class position once they leave it), are the closest to their clients in terms of attributes; thus a logical source of obtaining such agents is to train people from a culture the change agency is trying to affect[10].

In this classical approach to producing extension agents, there are the usual constraints of time and money, but its benefits justify the investment.

Again, there is the need for specially trained extension agents who have the basic intelligence to function within an innovative change agency, as well as the empathy and desire to work well with subsistence clients in rural areas. Without the best-trained staff available for this interface function between change-agency representative and client, the program may well be lost no matter how good the change agency and its administration.

I don't mean to imply that producing the kind of extension agent that is needed is a quick, inexpensive process. Considerable investment in education facilities and faculty will be necessary. Students would need, in addition to agronomy and engineering training, specialized course work in human-relations theory, psychology, and anthropology. Such an approach (which has already been initiated with graduate students at Mexico's National School of Agriculture at Chapingo) produces a superb extension agent, and while the cost both in time and money is high in the short run, in the long run, because larger numbers of clients can be effectively serviced, it becomes less prohibitive. Costs could be reduced by utilizing a special series of seminars and workshops with existing extension agents, but one would expect that the results in this stopgap approach would be somewhat lacking. That the investment in the training of this cadre of people will be costly cannot be denied; however, no serious developmentalist has recently suggested that there are any cheap solutions to the problems involved in rural development.[11]

In any case, the extension model will continue to play a primary role in development. In applying it to a volunteer system, new problems are bound to arise; but nevertheless, I envision a development approach that will use groups in the role of extension agents, working with counterparts in host countries. That would be costly indeed if paid professionals were used. However, already highly skilled volunteers—those with extensive training and cross-cultural experience, such as ex–Peace Corps volunteers—could serve as trainers for the world-development groups, thus keeping the cost of training very low. It all depends on how we coordinate and organize such activities.

Now one significant difference between the classical and the volunteer developmental efforts is the nature of the agent's responsibility and the technical means by which she or he interacts with fellow group members and recipients. In present-day Third World extension efforts, the agent's primary responsibility is to satisfy the home organization, which may not be all that interested in helping people. Also the agent may be inadequately trained (and in developing countries, this is all too often true). But even when the agent is adequately trained, she or he often finds organizational restrictions on what can be done— particularly so when that work extends into the political arena or into areas of development that the home organization will not support (even if it is appropriate to the people's needs).

The volunteer world extension agent's advantage will be that she or he is an autonomous agent responsible to a volunteer supporting and coordinating agency that espouses the view of serving people first. These agencies will not exercise the political and philosophical restraints of a more classic developmental agency because they will have none of the traditional coercive controls that go with working for money. Consequently, the volunteer agent will be working with a loose network of other volunteers whose joint philosophical orientation will be toward serving people—not organizational objectives.

Training, then, will focus on providing the agent with informational resources to maximize her or his effectiveness as a developmental group organizer. Since these extension agents will come from all parts of the world, it should be relatively easy to ensure that they will not be co-opted by any particular organization in a specific country; and since they will receive nothing in pay, the supporting information agencies will have no means of coercing volunteers to behave in accordance with political objectives.

## THE WORLD EXTENSION AGENT

A world development will require volunteers who understand the cultures of the people that their development groups are serving. Anybody with a sincere desire to volunteer her or his service, and is an empathy toward the people served, can be trained to be a development volunteer. But without a close knowledge of the culture in which she or he is working, it will take some time for that person's service to become effective. In this regard, then, ex–Peace Corps volunteers could furnish the shock troops of global development, supplying the first run of world extension agents.

Certainly, the literature of the National Council of Returned Peace Corps Volunteers (NCRPCV) is heading in that direction when it suggests that returned volunteers mobilize and continue their service in some capacity after returning to their home communities. For example, the organization's newsletter describes community efforts such as the High School Global Awareness Program—an AIDS awareness campaign staffed by ex-volunteers who worked in the primary African AIDS countries—and the creation of a regional network of returned volunteers in every state that can be called to action whenever the need for their international and organizational expertise arises.[12] At this time, there is an ex–Peace Corps volunteer living either in or within twenty miles of every community throughout the United States.

Consequently, it may well be that ex–Peace Corps volunteers

(not only of the United States—for Germany, the Soviet Union, England, and Japan also have Peace Corps programs) will be the logical source of recruits for the first generation of world extension agents. Not only are they empathetic to the concerns and objectives of a world development, but they also have the deep cultural knowledge and organizational experience to match their commitment.

The use of ex–Peace Corps volunteers as the first generation of global agents and as the trainers of others is in keeping with the U.S. Peace Corps statement of mission, which in part expects volunteers "to live peace, and to labor for peace from the beginning of their service to the rest of their lives."[13]

In the rotational scheme suggested earlier as a way of reducing the abuse of power by individual group members, and as other members of the development groups become knowledgeable in the host country's culture and in the skills of effective organizing, then the ex–Peace Corps agent/trainer can step aside until her or his turn as trainer comes around again, or else may go off to establish another working group.

Thus, not only are ex–Peace Corps volunteers used to establish the extension vehicle, they also serve as the first generation of global educators and trainers. This is a service totally consistent with the objectives of the parent organization.

The irony in thus utilizing ex–Peace Corps volunteers is that, during their original service, they were in the same shoes as extension agents in the traditional development agencies, for they had to satisfy the political demands of the U.S. government. In the 1960s when I was a volunteer, the government suffered from an obsession with making sure that it was not sending abroad student radicals from the various campus organizations of that time. And even today, if a volunteer does not follow all the rules and procedures established by the Peace Corps bureacracy, that volunteer will be in serious trouble.

Actually, this disillusionment regarding the political restrictions placed on them is what makes the network of ex–Peace Corps volunteers such a valuable resource as the first generation of global extension trainers. They already know that politically controlled, bureacracy-based international development agencies are ineffective in servicing basic human needs. That's a healthy understanding to impart to new volunteers, and can also help in the prevention of abusive administrative behavior within the volunteer movement.

Coming to the aid of this new generation of world extension agents and the groups they train is a rapidly evolving technology that will improve their effectiveness at an increasingly low cost. Trainers and their groups can access an extensive worldwide source of technical information. In fact, communications satellites and computerized information-search procedures will supply not only information, but also an audio means of contact among the extension agent and development groups and the project's recipients—eliminating the necessity of traveling to the host country. In fact, the agents of development can operate from their own homes, never physically visiting the people or countries they serve. The potential of this is truly exciting; Chapter 6 further explores the technical options of the world extension agent and her or his interaction with development groups around the globe.

We can begin a prototype effort today with even a limited number of trainers, and it looks as though ex–Peace Corps volunteers (through the NCRPCV) can serve as the first-generation shock troops for such a global development effort. But for the long-run, there will have to be a considerable change in the way the general population is educated. Today's nineteenth-century educational approaches will not do in an integrated world; and if we would sustain a volunteer world development, we will need more than the 13,000 ex–Peace Corps workers.

## EDUCATION, ORGANIZATION, AND WORLD DEVELOPMENT

The task of organizing a volunteer world development will require the backing of a supportive world citizenry. Ideally, the various educational systems of all the nations would work together in fostering that support. However, the system of education in the United States—to name one important source of support—has become so sloppy and undisciplined that the vast majority of its graduates are prepared for little more than a nineteenth-century style of blue-collar work, let alone the moral enterprise of creating a new world.

The world's industrial production systems are clearly in transition, and are becoming more and more information and automation based. What few workers will be required in the blue-collar positions of the twenty-first century will have to be highly skilled and trained technicians. Fortunately, there have at least been a few success stories in the U.S. rust belt. Some smaller companies have evolved with the times, and are now able to compete with Japan and Korea. These companies rely on the use of small groups, participative decision making, and a considerably higher skill level than was acceptable in the past.

The prognosis for the United States is that, because of the current outcry against the dismal state of U.S. education, we will make the changes necessary to produce an effective information-based work force (and maybe in time for the early twenty-first century). Actually, the current reaction is not unlike what followed the Soviet Union's Sputnik successes in the 1950s. I know how that affected me and my generation: Almost instantly, engineering and science became as fashionable as football and drag racing (and some of us tried to pursue all four at once).

There are two possible routes by which we can change the skill and attitude orientation of the U.S. work force. The first and most important route will be—as just noted—to follow through on improving and expanding the education offered by the public school system. We are finding, however, that the discipline of the family may be the most important variable. And it is again the Japanese who illustrate the power of the family. Class sizes in Japanese schools average close to fifty, and the physical plant is primitive—but Mama makes sure that the kids perform. In the United States, unfortunately, the family element is the most difficult to affect, and this will be discussed in Chapter 7. The second possible route to change would be in the direction of Vonnegut's *Player Piano*: to set up a totally automated, robot-maintained economic system where the people—basically ignorant and uneducated—are wards of the state and function primarily as consumers. While this latter route is technically a possibility, I believe and hope that the basic philosophical underpinnings of the United States would prevent its becoming an actuality.

What we may wind up with, though, is a hybrid of the two possibilities. We could ultimately see a First World in which individuals are supplied with everything they need by an automated economic system. But hopefully these same people will be educated to think in terms of—and to act on—spreading those benefits to the rest of the world. In effect, as a consequence of their conditioned schooling, First World citizens would believe that the redistribution of wealth and technology (the inherited right of all the world's citizens, as the Group of 77 put it) is their country's job—and, that is, their job. This orientation of the First World and its citizens would provide volunteer development organizations with the support they need to create the new world, and would be an important element in carrying the development process to its ultimate egalitarian goal: a global society in which all people are equal, and all people work for each other.

The behavioral technology does exist by which we could effect a new world development through the educational system (see Chapter 7). It may not seem so possible now, but this will change as we realize that the school curriculum for our children in a global economic system must give those children not only an understanding but also a sense of responsibility toward all citizens of the world. Really, we have no choice. To redevelop the educational system rationally and in terms of world society, the priority must be on an internalized concern for helping others at the first elementary as well as the most advanced levels of instruction.

## CONCLUDING REMARKS

It is not unreasonable to think of developing organizations that can carry out a volunteer world development. One must remain vigilant, however, lest the volunteer effort become as tyrannical and irrelevant as many of the professional development organizations have become. Volunteer organizations will therefore need to utilize participative structures; hierarchial, antidemocratic organizational forms will do us no good in the twenty-first century, and will not promote a world development.

Brute force, torture, and threat of physical deprivation no longer work the motivational wonders they once did.

Historically, the first nation to break the bonds of a hierarchial political system was the United States when it declared its independence from the English monarchy, and introduced to the world a democratic political system based on the wishes of the people. While that citizen-elected and -controlled system has certainly experienced its ups and downs, it has been the pathfinder for all of the anticolonialist as well as technological revolutions that have taken place since 1776. As such it would be logical for the United States to lead the way as a democratic, participative government that complements the volunteer world-development effort. Unfortunately, the United States will most likely not play that leadership role, for—while the Soviet bloc countries seem to be loosening up and becoming less centralized and autocratic in control of their people—the United States seems to becoming more centralized and less democratic.

One disappointing reality of our failure to recognize the value of democratic processes in carrying out creative endeavors is that the society now in the spotlight for promoting democracy as a means of resolving not only domestic but also international problems is the Soviet Union. This was highlighted in a speech recently given at a conference in Omaha by Oleg Derkousky of the Soviet Embassy (see also Chapter 2).[14]

Derkousky talked of the Soviet Union's return to common sense in foreign policy—its recognition that ideological efforts at the expense of democracy make things bad not only for the Third World, but for the Second as well. He went on to say that "Capitalism and Socialism will continue to develop on their own, but they intersect at the point of assuring human survival . . . Consequently it becomes dysfunctional to continue working for a class struggle because common human values must predominate over ideology."[15] If the Soviets are recognizing the predominance of common human values, then hopefully there will be a reduction of strife in existing regional conflicts throughout the Third World, and efforts initiated to prevent new ones. Let's all hope that they are serious.

Derkousky maintained that Soviet citizens, the press, and academics are now all permitted to contribute to a free flow of ideas—thus helping to formulate Soviet foreign policy. He stressed that participation is present at all levels in the process.

Let's assume that this is really happening. When was the last time you can remember having directly influenced this country's foreign policy? Analyzing the behavior of U.S. administrations throughout the Cold War, one can't help but notice that much of our foreign policy at that time was being formulated just as it was in the Soviet Union—behind closed doors. One thing that the Soviets are quite correctly now showing is how much we Americans have given up of our democratic political heritage in the past forty years. If we want to play a significant role in both the global economic system as well as world development in the years to come, we will have to take a closer look at our political practices, and come back from the antidemocratic adventures of especially the past decade.

Oleg Derkousky would like to see a future in which the Soviet Union and the United States work together on resolving regional conflicts and jointly aid the Third World, instead of using these countries as pawns in their world-scale ideological dispute. Such diplomatic cooperation can be only good news for the volunteer development effort. It would enable volunteers to interface with the institutional resources of both powers—particularly so if those two nations reduce their military budgets and redirect that capital to the support of volunteer development programs. And if we accept the possibility of a very close coordination between the two nations, then we can also expect there to be a synergistic effect in terms of logistical and resource support for volunteer projects.

One thing that the Cold War produced is a great number of transport vehicles and specialized housing facilities in the form of military bases and embassy compounds throughout the world. As noted in Chapter 3, the key to developing an effective volunteer effort is to provide vehicles and a place to crash so that the costs of transportation and lodging are controlled. Beyond those costs, volunteers can always get their own food and wash their own clothes. This, then, is what both the United States and the Soviets can supply: facilities for people who—while providing their expertise and time for free—would not have to bear the expenses of housing and transportation within

the country they are working. Additionally, the two governments could provide volunteers with flights to the host country
via military transports, or even put pressure on the private airlines to permit volunteer teams access to the vacant seats on
their international flights.

Through the McCollum Amendment, such use of military
transports is already available in the United States, and has been
used to transport civilians for emergency activities. This is a
precedent that could easily be expanded to benefit volunteer
world-development efforts.

To manage such a creative interface between the two governments, there must be a coordinating office maintained by volunteers who have the power to access resources from the two
governments as project teams and ideas are developed. Volunteers from the NCRPCV, for instance, could initiate this role—
and quite literally, out of their bedrooms or garages. That is to
say, a large number of ex-Peace Corps volunteers live in the
Washington, D.C., area. The coordination teams need not even
commute to the State Department, but could easily operate from
their homes by linking their PCs to the State Department
computers with a telephone modem. The State Department
computers—besides being a wealth of information on any given
country—could also routinely log the availability of vacant seats
on the private airlines and the military schedules. The coordination teams would then do the grunt work of linking the resources with the project teams.

A similar linkage could be established to connect with Soviet
volunteer counterparts. Communication between the American
coordinators and the Soviet office could be done at very low cost
through the VITA (Volunteers for International Technical
Assistance, based in Washington) satellite communications
system—a system designed to be operated out of a suitcase.

The point is that volunteers can effectively do the coordination
work, and do it in such a way as to avoid the institutional failings
of a professional bureaucracy. Given that international *glasnost*
is upon us and hopefully here to stay, conceptualizing such a
volunteer-based logistical system now makes sense. This combined with the advanced, low-cost communication technologies
coming on-line (discussed in greater detail in Chapter 6) provide

an opportunity for world development that couldn't even be dreamed about in earlier years.

Regardless of the technical details, however, the main thing is that any world development organization must include the Soviet bloc countries. Not only are their physical resources needed (and presumably, after reducing military expenditures, they too will have a surplus to commit to world development), but so is their support in reducing the regional conflicts that disrupt the progress of too many Third World countries.

For example, Premier Gorbachev of the Soviet Union in late 1989 told President Ortega of Nicaragua that the game was over: Only economic aid in the form of advisors and equipment that could not be used militarily would be forthcoming. Simultaneously, President Bush said the same thing to the Nicaraguan Contras. Peace developed in the region because the two central supportive players in that current conflict created a new environment to make it so.

In order for a volunteer-based world development to take place, we must continue to eliminate these wasteful Third World conflicts, 90 percent of which have been exacerbated by involvement of the superpowers. At the time of this writing, it looks like there may be a break in the ideological wars. Can it be that the two superpowers will cooperate enough to become allies in development of the rest of the world? This would probably all come crashing down, of course, were Mikhail Gorbachev to be purged from the Soviet picture. In that regard, those of us who are religious should be lighting candles for his survival.

As I have said before in many books and articles, the concise assessment for organizational change made by Warren Bennis in the late 1950s—"democracy is inevitable"—becomes more and more relevant each year. That this is being borne out by the Soviets and the Japanese in their current behavior is yet another affirmation of Bennis's original insight. The United States has a need to examine its own state of democracy. And it is just as important that hierarchical, autocratic structures be eliminated from the volunteer organizations of world development.

What we are finding, as one century winds down and we enter the next, is the opportunity to finally make a serious effort at world development. The experience base of ex-volunteers is there, the low-cost communications technology is coming, and the ideological conflict of the two major international powers seems to be toning down. All the organizational elements of a volunteer-controlled and -directed world development are coming together. Dare we be optimistic?

## NOTES

1. John Marshall, "Why the Israeli Army Wins," *Harper's* (October 1958).

2. R. Feigenbaum and P. McCorduck, *The Fifth Generation* (New York: Addison-Wesley, 1983).

3. C. Arndt and S. Everett, *Education for a World Society* (New York: Harper and Brooks, 1951).

4. Feigenbaum and McCorduck, *The Fifth Generation*.

5. *The MacNeil/Lehrer News Hour*, PBS Television, September 18, 1985.

6. Feigenbaum and McCorduck, *The Fifth Generation*.

7. Peter Drucker, *The Frontiers of Management* (New York: Truman Talley Books, 1986), pp. 320–324.

8. A. Jedlicka, *Organization for Rural Development* (New York: Praeger, 1977).

9. Ibid., p. 23.

10. Ibid., p. 25.

11. Ibid., p. 138.

12. *National Council of Returned Peace Corps Volunteers Newsletter*, December 1988.

13. Excerpted from the U.S. Peace Corps mission statement.

14. Oleg Derkousky, Address to the Ninth Annual Third World Conference, Omaha, Nebraska, October 1988.

15. Ibid.

# SIX

# Telecommunications and Institutional Support

That communications technology is rapidly advancing has been quite evident for the past decade. Even couch potatoes are aware that their Saturday afternoon football game is beamed live via geosynchronous satellite communications. In the near future, such systems will be backed up by fiberglass transoceanic cables that can handle an increasing volume of communications, as both corporations and private citizens expand their global connections.

Yet the very fast and increasingly cheap international communications that we so casually accept is extremely recent (less than twenty years). I well recall how difficult it was to call my parents from Bolivia when I was working there as a Peace Corps volunteer in 1967. I had to hunt out a ham radio operator willing to contact another operator in the States who might be willing to dial my parents from her or his private phone, so that my transmission from the shortwave system could be translated through the phone. Needless to say, the call was very scratchy and difficult to understand, and certainly not instantaneous. But it did work, and it was cheap.

By contrast, in 1982 I was working in the boondocks of Guinea-Bissau for several weeks. Guinea-Bissau, being the poorest country in Africa, was still then like the Bolivia of 1967 and had no civilian communications network—although, judging by the antennae and disks sprouting from the Soviet and U.S. embassies, the people in there were well outfitted. Short-term workers such as myself, however, had no access to those facilities except in the event that we should contract some horrible disease or be facing death in an imminent revolution. In any case, I stepped across into a really grubby little border town of Senegal, where I was able to walk up to a sidewalk telephone and use my charge number to call my family in Iowa in less than a minute. Although 1967 seems not so long ago, most of us take the tremendous changes since then rather for granted.[1]

Given that the cost of these connecting services continues to go down (almost monthly), the role that communications systems can play in volunteer development programs becomes increasingly relevant. One variable that can either hinder or promote any development effort is the ability of the assisting groups to communicate cheaply and effectively with the people they wish to assist. And without controlling for that most basic of variables, one cannot seriously propose a workable development through volunteerism.

To be more specific, let's consider forming an effective volunteer work group (presented briefly in Chapter 4) based in the United States. First of all, to get our volunteer group functioning within the donor country would depend totally on a constant stream of communications, especially given that we Americans no longer live in "nuclear" city environments (which reflect a twelfth-century vision of the world, anyway). It is a reality to be reckoned with in creating a world development that volunteers will more often than not come from the highly educated, high-income bracket of the urban population, and from among rural people. One characteristic of this resource base is that such people do not live in central locations (such as one finds with the underclass in, say, Harlem). "Bill" may live on a farm twenty miles out of town; "Sue" may be in a wooded area ten miles away; and so on. Right from the start, then, the telephone acts as a key organizational tool, allowing these people to plan, coordinate, and interact with each other. Without it, the project would never get together in the first place.

But with the phone, they can arrange meetings, discuss preliminary concerns, and hash out disagreements. In the end, their face-to-face contact turns out to be largely an affirmation of all the legwork that took place before the meeting. Still, the need for communication is no less significant when they get into the international phase of the project. If anything, it becomes even more important then, because of the inevitable difficulties involved in conveying ideas to an audience that doesn't really think the same. In any case, instant communications throughout the planning process is a must. This is where present and soon-to-be-acquired communication technologies can play such an integrating role in the volunteer development effort.

One technology now being implemented is VITA's Third World communications satellite system.[2] While antiquated when compared to the state-of-the-art systems now circling the globe because it uses a 1960s style of digital transmission, the VITA satellite nevertheless has three compelling virtues: It is available to any volunteer group that wants to link up; it is provided free or at cost; and it can be operated basically out of a suitcase by anybody who has had a minimum of training in the system.

Operating on ham frequencies, the entire system—complete with printout machine—is contained in a medium-size suitcase that can be carried wherever it is needed. For volunteer groups in the States, this means that, when volunteer group A needs to communicate with members of project A in country C, they can do so out of their living rooms in the course of conducting a group meeting. Extension agent D in country C, who may happen to be driving somewhere in the bush at the time the group decides to contact him, will stop and—tapping off his car battery—talk with his counterparts in the States.

Immediacy of feedback between development group and client country is central to being able to clarify and resolve communication dilemmas as they arise (rather than waiting for a letter or telegram). Again, this is nothing so very revolutionary: Embassies, military forces, and large corporations have long had such a capability. What is revolutionary is its affordability—a key requisite under the shoestring budgets of most volunteer development efforts.

The near future in communications (that is, 1990s) looks even more exciting, as well as affordable, for volunteer groups. We can anticipate that low-cost instant translators (already in prototype stage) will be available at a reasonable price. In fact, the technology is advancing so fast that the translators may even soon be simulating the senders' voices. With increasing minia- turization, it may not be so farfetched to imagine translating communication boxes being implanted in the larynx should one decide to be so dramatic.

Thus, the breakthrough in computer technology can control for yet another difficult variable in international development work: language. This is especially true given the abysmal con- dition of U.S. education, in which virtually nobody—even the college educated—acquires a proficiency in foreign languages. Not understanding the recipient country's language can be a severe hindrance to any assistance project.

"Okay, gang, we're going to work with a project in Southern Nigeria," decides the "Merle Hay" team in West Des Moines, Iowa, "so slip in the Ibo language cartridge in the old voice translator, link up with the VITA computer, and you're ready to begin serving mankind."

Well, we all know it's not quite that easy. As Chapter 5 sug- gested, you've also got to have organization—and, unfortu- nately, something that looks like bureaucracy.

## AN IN-COUNTRY LINKING OF PEOPLE WITH DEVELOPMENT PROJECTS

Before one can utilize the available telecommunications tech- nology that will enable First and Second World groups to com- municate with Third World counterparts, there must be a systematic means of developing donor-country project groups and linking them with international project field sites. Unfor- tunately, while such a system can certainly be developed (and to some extent already is, by the NCRPCV), it also requires the creation of a limited bureaucracy—a bureaucracy that, because it is volunteer managed, should not get out of control. Today's personal computers and tomorrow's voice-actuated computers easily provide the technology to establish, maintain, and mon- itor a network of people, groups, and field sites. An example will help explain how this may come about.

Many organizations such as church groups, community-sponsored groups, and national organizations such as the NCRPCV already engage in development activities with specific countries. For example, in my own community in Iowa, the First Christian Church has sponsored efforts to drill potable water wells in Guatemala. Members paid their own way, and the work in selected villages was backed up logistically by the church's local field mission office. There are probably hundreds of these projects that have been carried out on an ad-hoc, uncoordinated basis throughout the United States. The problem with such a scatter-gun approach is that, while it can be very effective at the micro level, its macro effect is nil because it has not been incorporated into a systematic, overall development strategy.

Moreover, the opportunity for projects to be carried out simultaneously is prevented when the different organizations are not aware of each other. In shoestring volunteer efforts, one needs to be concerned about maximizing results. For example, when the Cedar Falls, Iowa, First Christian Church teams went to Guatemala, it may be that there was also a Catholic team from Sausalito, California, wanting to establish a milk supplement program for village children, but with no travel resources within the community to carry out that effort. Had the First Christian people been in contact or aware of the Catholics' concern, it might have been relatively easy for the well-drilling teams also to carry out the milk supplement effort. Then, too, there is a synergistic effect that is a spin-off of establishing a network, as one becomes aware of what is available, where it is, and how it can be added to one's own efforts. This does, however, require at least a minimum coordinating bureaucracy.

Logistically, this information and coordination activity could be handled by volunteer operators. The first step would be to log all the groups throughout a given donor country that already are or have expressed an interest in working on projects in the Third World. But let me back up a moment. In the preliminary effort to coordinate a volunteer world development, there will need to be a national organization, at least, that can put the coordinating mechanism together as well as provide a corps of dedicated and experienced people. Members of the NCRPCV meet all the basic requirements. They have proved their basic commitment to serve, already have international field experience, and would no doubt be willing to play the role of the extension trainer (as presented in Chapter 5). They are the experienced vets who would be continuing to pursue a service for the world in their communities after completing active field duty, as prescribed by the Peace Corps mission.

The interesting quality of the NCRPCV is that it has organized itself nationally to the extent that at least one returned Peace Corps volunteer lives either in or within twenty miles of every community in the United States. These people can certainly play a key role in organizing local development teams, logging information about what these teams are doing and what they want to do, and—most importantly for both national and international coordination—logging the specific skills, past experience, and availability of its members into the development team's PC. By telephone modem, this information can in turn be stored in a global network computer so that other countries, project teams, and volunteer development organizations can access and establish the availability of people they may need for a specific project.

Unfortunately, this does all boil down to yet another bureaucracy. But having an informed awareness of the potential evil within them, these volunteer bureaucracies can design themselves to prevent it from developing. Actually, a specific knowledge of people's experience and skills becomes a critical component of such preventive measures, along with an understanding on the part of the members of the network that they may never get to go to the country they are helping (not in their role as development volunteers, that is). They will be doing all their work in-country (in their home country), and communicating with host-country counterparts through the satellite communications system. And if the need should happen to arise for their presence there, they would be paying for their own flight (or possibly be flown as cargo in a military transport). And in this eventuality of travel, again, they could expect no more than a place to crash with kitchen facilities. Not paying people has a direct bearing on the quality of commitment applied to developmental work. Being paid nothing, one cannot resent being paid too little, nor need one endure any degree of abrasive, totalitarian managerial control. When there is no payment, then the threat of dismissal or monetary punishment can have no effect. This is immensely appealing in a volunteer system. With no means of punishing, punishment cannot become a means of control, and one must rely on a participative working together to get things done.

Let's return to that Merle Hay team in West Des Moines, Iowa. In the year 2000 it's quite possible that its team members will be able to slip their Ibo cartridges into their voice translators; but in 1990 they still need someone who can speak Ibo, if they want to communicate with their counterparts. By making a computer search, they may find a woman in Fredericksburg, Texas, who served a two-year tour in Nigeria and speaks fluent Ibo. Furthermore, while it might be difficult for her to travel to Iowa, she can still serve as the team translator by linking her home phone with the group's satellite transmitter. Then when the team needs some other specific skill, the members again do a computer search, find someone who has the needed skill (this person may live in Newark, New Jersey), and incorporate that person into the team's effort. Although these people may never actually see one another, through the low-cost telecommunications systems their various skills and experiences can be coordinated into teams that tackle specific development projects. The key, as stated earlier, is a reasonably well organized national or international group that can serve as a volunteer-directed coordinating agency. The NCRPCV looks very much like it could be the pioneer in taking this first step toward world development.

Another innovation—thanks to the new communications satellites that relay KU transmission frequencies—is the addition of low-cost visual transmission. The advantage of KU frequencies is that they are very low-power signals. In earlier years the technology was not sophisticated enough to handle low-power transmission; therefore it was necessary to use high-voltage, big-booster systems with large dishes.[3] Such systems worked fine, but the cost of the system as well as the power demands and the sheer size of all the equipment put them out of reach of low-budget programs. Systems that work the KU frequencies require very little power to operate; household current will suffice. The equipment is suitcase sized, the dish transmitter/receiver reduced to pizza size, and the cost of operation similarly diminished. And with KU transmission, even visual communications will soon be sent very cheaply.

At the present time, there is already a fairly cheap, but less sophisticated, visual transmission system—Panasonic's image phone unit—which transmits black-and-white frames over conventional phone systems at the rate of one frame every eight seconds (causing a visual time lapse as you talk to your counterpart). But continuous visual—while available through the major communications companies—is still very expensive. That will all change as the KU frequencies come on-line in the mid–1990s. Since the new devices will be aggressively promoted by the Japanese companies that are leading the R&D and are trying— as they always do—to capture the long-term market, one would expect that, in addition to their being derived from a less expensive technology, they will also be made artificially cheaper by international competition.

Well, inexpensive visual communication, especially if combined with high definition television transmission will add a whole new dimension to volunteer work. (High definition television—another technological sector being aggressively pursued by the Japanese—provides a clarity of picture that is almost three dimensional.)[4] The primary logistical and budget breaker in international work has been the expense involved in travel and lodging. In many future efforts, project members need never set foot within the country they serve because they will be able to do their work over the communications systems at home.

Consider the following scenario: Probably sometime around the year 2000, a group of farmers in Dutchess County, New York, are working with a counterpart group in Costa Rica. Using their voice translators (since, in this case, none of the former speak Spanish), they work out the basic parameters of the counterpart's agricultural problem (say, improving the amount of organic matter in the soil). As the problem is further defined, the New York group realizes that they need a visual inspection of the soil. They switch on the high definition transmitter and instruct the counterparts on how to get a representative soil sample from the fields. The counterparts lay out their collected samples in front of the camera. Because of the almost natural, three-dimensional quality of the transmission, the New York group—relying on their own years of farming experience—can tell by the color and by the tilth (as the counterparts run their fingers through the soil) the basic nature of the soil problem, and then discuss among themselves what should be done to resolve it. Incidentally, this sort of TV diagnosis is already practiced by medical doctors, both internationally and within isolated parts of the world. It's very expensive, but also very effective. In a similar manner, volunteer experts will be able to provide their expertise to other countries very cheaply, and very quickly.

When it comes time for the New York farmers to discuss solutions with their Costa Rican counterparts, high definition television can show the kind of soil that it is possible to produce by corrective actions. If the adding of organic matter is prescribed, then the project team can illustrate how to build a compost pile, how to manage it, and how to incorporate it into the soil. In fact, the advisors can even supervise the counterparts building their own compost piles, tell them what they are doing right and what they are doing wrong, as well as show them all the associated activities that go into doing the job correctly— even though the advisors are sitting in someone's living room in Beacon, New York. And the communication goes both ways— the composting procedures being adjusted for the Costa Rican conditions of temperature and humidity, say. Of course, this scenario can be repeated for virtually any kind of project, once the communications systems are on line.

This, I think, is the breakthrough that will facilitate a volunteer world development. It will be no longer necessary even to leave one's home to participate directly in helping other people in other cultures and countries (and for all those health benefits talked about in Chapter 1). In fact, in this high-tech cum low-cost scenario, even disabled people can contribute their skills directly and see the benefits of their help, even though the recipients be 10,000 miles away. And though the participants in these projects may never meet each other in person, they do come to know each other through their visual contact (which, in the early twenty-first century, will probably improve even more through low-cost hologram transmissions.)

## SYSTEMS AND SATISFACTIONS

This technology-enhanced kind of volunteering has the advantages of immediacy and participation. When people give money to development organizations, they get a picture of the child that they're helping as well as an occasional letter translated by some organization employee. People in the programs described in this book will be directly giving of their skills and their time (as well as their money, no doubt) to benefit increasingly familiar recipients in other parts of the world, for specific purposes they mutually determine. Consequently, the donors know exactly who they are giving to and what purpose they are serving. They need fear no bureaucratic laundering of their contributions, which in some of the most notorious international-help programs can result in more than half of the contributions going to administration and advertising services.

This point cannot be too greatly emphasized. One problem discussed primarily in Chapter 4 is that participation in our democracy-based institutions has been taken away from most of us. We have been reduced to a passive acceptance of representation in government, service, and even our philanthrophy. (Look at the "professionalism" manifested by the international development organizations that solicit our help with TV presentations of starving babies.) In a global democracy—which is basic to a world development in the twenty-first century—all citizens who desire to do so must be allowed to participate directly. Only then can we build a commitment that will sustain development efforts over the long run. Group participation is the essential ingredient that will free not only our brothers and sisters in other countries, but ourselves as well.

It is in this sense, then, that an interactive and participative visual communications system would promote a true new-world development while simultaneously satisfying that basic need within us to help others. Visual devices that allow us to see and know those we are helping in other countries can only be considered to be—as Jeremy Bentham would say—for the greater good. Certainly it would enhance that pleasure we experience in helping others.

Maybe there's a little bit (at least) of Jesus in each of us, after all—referring to the Campbellian hypothesis that Jesus' self-sacrifice on the cross was his bliss (or his peak experience, as Abraham Maslow would have it). Joseph Campbell mentions that one of the scriptures describes Jesus dancing in the Garden before his capture, when he knew that his final bliss was near.[5] In the ultimate sacrifice of himself, Jesus achieved the final purpose that he believed he served: to establish a religion focused on loving (and helping) one's neighbor as oneself. That humanity hasn't yet matched his bliss in sacrifice doesn't negate the value of his message. Believe it or not (and this may be hard to believe, given the presently abysmal state of human relations), many people do actually behave toward others as Jesus would have them behave. And they recommend it highly.

Volunteer behavior may actually turn out to be a natural part of all human beings, once the cultural myths that train people to consider the residents of other cultures as something less than human are removed. The Sioux, for instance, felt that they were the only human beings. Similarly, we were taught to view Soviet citizens as godless and brutish (when, in fact, religion seems to be stronger there—in spite of Soviet dogma—than in the United States). The underlying human psyche (that is, the animal nature so willing to sacrifice self for the species) must be yearning to come forth. Maybe we are now reaching a point in human evolution where we can remove those cultural blinders that impare our understanding of and desire to help other cultures, and get on with the business of enabling our brothers and sisters to share equally in the Gaian fecundity of Mother Earth. Given that the church is no longer in a position to create that kind of world citizen, the responsibility will probably devolve to the education system. That behavioral route to global change will be discussed in Chapter 7.

## THE PRACTICAL SIDE OF HANDLING VISUAL SYSTEMS

A question may have occurred to the reader as to who will handle all the high-tech equipment on the Third World end. True, volunteers in the developed countries would already largely have the understanding—and in some cases, the equipment—to handle the latest mode of communications, while it is likely that peasant farmers would not. The answer is to use the existing network of international workers spread throughout the world. This is comprised of Peace Corps volunteers (not only of the United States, but also of the Soviet Union, Europe, and Japan), Maryknoll fathers, Mennonite volunteers, and all the other thousands of international field workers out there, constantly rotating around the earth. They are an overhead expense of their respective countries and home organizations, and are a global resource just waiting to be tapped and directed together as logistical backup for all those armchair volunteers in the home countries. And the armchair volunteers can then be actively engaged in development via the international communications networks, even if they never actually enter the countries in which they work.

As an example, let's return to those farmers in Dutchess County, New York, working with the group in Costa Rica. Costa Rica still has a Peace Corps office. The Peace Corps volunteers in Costa Rica could serve as equipment operators for the project's visual communications system. During the volunteers' in-country training, they would have to be taught how to use the communication devices, as well as receive a better training in small-group organization and participative approaches to joint decision making. Having worked as a Peace Corps trainer, I know that some training is already provided in group skills, but for the most part, it's rather primitive. Given the Peace Corps' penchant for training, however, that situation could easily be changed if a commitment toward such collaborative programs were made.

The volunteer in the field would be computer linked to development teams in the States, and assigned the responsibility of working with them. Of course, having the communication equipment, she or he would also be able to take care of any backup work necessary before the actual field work was carried out with the assorted village groups.

Consequently, the communication activity itself would be relatively straightforward. The field volunteer would have talked with the stateside group before determining what the day's activities would be. Arriving at the village, she or he meets with the corresponding village group leaders to present what the volunteer team felt should be the day's agenda and to set up the transmission equipment. Then, should computer translators or a team translator not be available, the field volunteer translates to both groups of people—the Costa Rican farmers and the Dutchess County team, say—as they jointly work on the problem.

Now certain additional things could be done to enhance this process, and they are consistent with the Peace Corps' efforts to tailor the skills of volunteers to the needs of the host-country participants. Instead of sending a B.A. generalist into this particular situation (an extremely common practice in the 1960s)—who might be high on communication skills and empathy, but very low on agricultural skills—a volunteer with some actual agronomy training could be provided. What this would mean is that, if the Dutchess County farmers needed a simple soil test or needed to explain relatively complex agricultural explorations in a manner comprehensible to the local farmers, the agronomy-trained volunteer would be able to handle it. This is not to disparage the B.A. generalist: She or he can serve very well—just not so well as the agronomy-trained volunteer.

Once our soil-problem village had been served, the volunteer would go on to the next—down-linking with yet another in-country team. In this case, it might be a group of retired weapons engineers from China Lake, California, working with a village on low-cost solar dehydrators. This linkage process would continue throughout the day until our volunteer had finished with his case load.

I use the example of a Peace Corps volunteer because it is the field agency with which I am most familiar. But certainly, field workers from the Maryknoll order of Catholic priests and nuns, the Mennonite missions, CARE, and the other hundred or so uncoordinated international programs that exist in this and other countries would serve as well. The point to remember is that—as argued in Chapter 4—the service must be performed by volunteer, unpaid, participative labor so as to eliminate the institutional jockeying for power and control and to prevent the development of the bureaucratic abuses common to the traditional international aid programs.

## HOW TRADITIONAL DEVELOPMENT SOURCES
## CAN HELP

A consistent theme of this book has been to avoid like the plague the controls, excesses, and lack of involvement by recipients that come with the bureaucratically controlled development approach. Campbell is quite right when he describes the bureaucrat as one who has not fully developed as a human—who lives in terms of an imposed system.[6] Yet realistically, at least in the early decades of a volunteer-directed world development effort, there will be involvement with traditional bureaucracies. There will be an involvement not only with the bureaucracies of the traditional international-development system, but also with the educational bureaucracies that provide the training of each new generation. Just because bureaucracies are more often than not flawed organizational systems that have become archaic and dysfunctional to the development of a global community does not mean that volunteers cannot work with them in effecting a volunteer-controlled world development.

In a speech at the 1988 Third World development conference in Omaha, Kenneth Bleakley of the U.S. State Department made a semi-impassioned plea for more creative efforts in world development.[7] His suggestions included volunteer workers (not the low-paid employee type of the Peace Corps, but real volunteers) having access to resources of certain government agencies such as the State Department. He gave no specific examples of what could be done, but I have a few ideas, some of which were introduced in Chapter 5.

Given the great amount of surplus equipment and all the transport activities that go on in the military (which by definition is almost all logistics), there is much that could be creatively accessed from this source. For example, the Air Force has a lot of planes flying all over the world. One of the routine things that the Air Force does is to fly commissary supplies to the various embassies. Yes, indeed, not only does the Air Force deliver nuclear bombs: It also delivers turkeys. Suffice it to say that the efficiency of this delivery system is not high. There is often plenty of room to stow an extra passenger or two. And why not carry along volunteers who are going to work in a specific country, especially aboard routine flights that have no military secrecy attached to them? Certainly, this is within the realm of the possible and has even been done before—on a small scale—under the McCollum Act, which allows military planes to be used by civilians in emergency situations within the United States.

Certainly the McCollum Act could be utilized to even greater efficiency if a volunteer logistics team were allowed to link its computers to the Air Force's unclassified-transport logistical system. That way the volunteer group would have a continuous reading on what planes were going where, and how much available space could be filled by volunteers going to certain countries.

One may think that this could never happen because the military would never submit to it—and that probably would have been true twenty years ago. But, despite the reactionism of the Reagan years, there are many ways in which our government and military forces are now more open to an interface with civilian forces. It is quite reasonable to imagine this kind of coordination between civilian volunteers and the military. (After all, in the ultimate educational process, all military personnel will have undergone the same kind of global involvement training as the rest of the population, and thus will have an internalized concern for an equitable world. (This is discussed in Chapter 7.) There is also now an actual precedent for this kind of interface: the collaboration of military research facilities with civilians who need access to their information, as has occurred under the Stevensen-Struever Act of 1981.

Under this act, military research centers are required to make all their unclassified research (research that has not been restricted for national security reasons) available through computerized retrieval systems that any civilian can access to look for research that may be relevant to her or his own private or commercial activities. Once something has been found, the civilian can actually obtain the details and results of that research (many times for free). To support this interplay, the military R&D centers have to allocate 0.5 percent of their budgets to the computer retrieval systems and provide personnel to manage them. And it isn't necessarily all esoteric research. While military

R&D does produce cruise missiles, it also produces composting toilets, photovoltaic electrical generators, and improved food-processing technologies. These latter designs are all unclassified and available for civilian search and retrieval.

So the idea of going one step further and being more closely involved in the logistics of military flights is really only consistent with the Stevensen-Struever Act. Sending five agricultural volunteers to Costa Rica with the embassy's Thanksgiving turkeys is something that could be easily arranged if a volunteer coordinating group had access to the schedule of routine Air Force flights and permission to route volunteers through them. It would in no way compromise the security of this country and in fact might even enhance it, by showing that the United States can also manage to use its high-dollar, rapid-obsolescence technology as a resource for peace. And if our tax dollars are going to pay for the turkey flights anyway, why not maximize those dollars by lending logistical support to the world-development effort, utilizing what is basically a military overhead expense anyway? The price is right on all accounts: The coordinating would be done entirely by the volunteers, who would log the Air Force schedules and send them to development groups throughout the country so that cues for sending people to field sites could be established and carried out.

And let's not stop with just the military. Civilian transport agencies (both passenger and freight) also have excess capacity that should be made available to volunteers who are traveling across nations. A computer linkage with the volunteer travel agency could again be established to put field workers on the flights to project countries as spare seats open up. And the commercial companies would no doubt find advantage in the arrangement, too—using their involvement for advertising purposes. "See what Pan Am did last year? Sent free of charge 2,000 volunteers to work for world peace and development." If the pendulum swings and the trend of the 1990s turns out to be a concern for the rest of the world, then such advertising will be a sign of the times.

There are also currently many useful resources that are leftovers of the Cold War: In 1989, some 85 military bases were being closed (and more to come). Just think of all the material resources associated with those bases. Telecommunications equipment, trucks, computers, and even canned and dried food rations—much of which (if we can believe what we see on television) tends to be destroyed, rather than salvaged. Certainly, a little creativity on the part of the State Department—which Mr. Bleakely in his speech in Omaha seemed to promise us would be forthcoming—is all that's needed to get volunteer salvagers in there sorting through that vast store of government-issue riches and rescuing what they can as backup for host-country projects. The Air Force could transport some of it. But for heavier equipment such as trucks—we won't need tanks or half-tracks—would it not be possible to call on the Navy and the Merchant Marine, as well as perhaps the huge shipping fleet operated by the Japanese (who are being increasingly pressured to help the Third World, and increasingly say they will do so)?

The answer, of course, is yes. Once you get a network functioning, its synergism can expand the movement dramatically, given proper leadership and an effective promotion. People and organizations line up to make their contributions—especially if the news media make it chic, and a few of the "beautiful people" become involved.

## WHAT EX–PEACE CORPS VOLUNTEERS ARE NOW DOING

Earlier I have suggested more than once that the Peace Corps could play a substantial role in the leadership of a volunteer world development. True to the dynamic climate of this arena in these times, that possibility is already being implemented by the NCRPCV, even as I write. Its December 1988 newsletter reports on a 24–hour Peace Corps vigil at President Kennedy's grave. (As for me personally, well, I recognize the importance of symbols. But it was Senator Hubert Humphrey who first originated the idea of the Peace Corps and who fought it through.) The event was described as follows:

This was the capstone event following our 24 hour vigil in the Capitol Rotunda. Every one of you who accepted the invitation from the National Council had the opportunity to share your reflections about what

Peace Corps meant to you, and to share it in that great hall of this nation. We are the only group in the history of the republic so honored for a full day, for so personal a task. And what it did, our Journals of peace, as well as honor the memory of our founder, was to have the country focus on the National Council as a separate entity. This is essential if we hope to be an effective and serious organization, moving ahead on our priority goals of educating Americans about the developing world, pressing for a more humane foreign policy, strengthening the Peace Corps itself.[8]

Well, that's pretty heady, if not a bit hokey—with the testimonials and all—but that's the way it goes. Just quietly doing the job without going through the PR doesn't seem to work at this point in human evolution. And besides—speaking of cultural symbols—we have done a lot worse than the image of middle-age ex–Peace Corps volunteers holding candles at Kennedy's grave and speaking from their hearts in the capitol rotunda. (Certain aerospace company ads in the not-so-distant past being a case in point. They showed B–52 crewmen pulling down their antiblast visors, and the caption beneath read, "Eat death, Comrades.")

In any case, as a consequence of its promotional venture, the NCRPCV has now received from Congress a Biden-Pell grant through which it can extend mini-grants to local groups for community-level educational efforts focusing on the Third World. Such efforts are intended to discover what will be needed to create a new world. In effect, then, the kind of volunteer group that I have been describing, and that can be mobilized for both domestic and international work, is already being established. At the moment, the Biden-Pell–sponsored effort concentrates on educating children about the need for a global awareness and primarily provides travel money for ex-volunteers who talk in local schools and help with curriculum development.[9]

Another interesting Corps spinoff is the network of groups throughout the country that call themselves the Friends of Peace Corps. In these "cells," too, ex-volunteers contribute their insights and manage projects directed toward the countries where they served as field volunteers. So things are already happening, and the coordinated efforts that I have suggested throughout this book to maximize effectiveness will no doubt come to pass, as well.

Peace Corps itself has become increasingly creative in its utilization of veteran talent, by directly recruiting ex-volunteers for short-term field assignments with the Corps. At this writing, I have received a request to join again for a six-to-twelve–month assignment teaching in the Philippines. For this, I would be paid expenses and a readjustment allowance of $200 for each month I served. Now, the $200 a month is meaningless, but the opportunity to serve again is enticing. And when such requests finally become tailored to, say, four-month opportunities (the time that academics have available during the summer), there will be thousands of people ready to answer the call.

This also suggests other ideas in terms of a follow-through on education projects, using satellite systems. Why couldn't there be a four-month internship in the education area for ex–Peace Corps volunteers that would, by design, be followed by a continued program via satellite? How would that work? Very simple. Assuming that the Peace Corps—or whatever agency—has already established an arrangement with a specific village and school system, the part-time volunteer would come in, serve the teaching internship, establish ties with key people and the student body, and then return to the States. There the volunteer would continue her or his teaching relationship with the community via satellite transmission from home during the evenings or on weekends—whatever scheduling is most workable on both ends. Remember again that KU satellite bands, small dish receivers, and less expensive communications devices in general will soon render this kind of program very reasonably priced. (And who knows? Maybe AT&T, say, would be willing to provide free transmission. Of course, it would get a great publicity plug for its generosity.)

The last point to be made here is that—as any ex–Peace Corps volunteer can tell you—once the development process does get turned on, synergism will keep it moving. There is an infectious quality to volunteerism. And its time does seem to have arrived. Maybe the "me only" cycle really has terminated and the 1960s are about to reincarnate. No matter that they now appear middle-aged and scarred enough to be called "mature." Given that the

Soviets are now working with us, maybe we are indeed headed for a kinder, gentler world where finally we will give peace a chance. So maybe the dawning of the age of Aquarius did turn a little chilly: That just gave us some time to cool down and become more effective leaders—time to think and design the new world that doesn't necessarily have to be so brave, but that does have to be fair and equitable to all its citizens. This is one sceptic who won't say nay.

## ONE FEDERALLY SPONSORED VOLUNTEER PROGRAM THAT FITS THE PARADIGM

One little-known federal program called the Volunteers in Overseas Cooperative Assistance (VOCA), which is administered by the U.S. Agency for International Development (AID), certainly fits within the paradigm of volunteer development efforts that I have proposed.

In this program, volunteers are recruited to provide short-term assistance for farm cooperatives and agricultural projects in the developing world. Typically their tours of duty run around four months—timed so that volunteer specialists can actually do something, without totally jeopardizing their work at home. Notice that this is consistent with the time period for initiating satellite education systems, proposed in the previous section. And—just as in Chapter 1 the health benefits of volunteerism were indicated, especially for those senior citizens who bring their life and technical skills to volunteering—"Many of those picked for overseas assignments are retired folks who are especially skilled or knowledgeable. . . . Their out-of-pocket expenses—food, lodging, transportation—are provided, but volunteers draw no salary."[10]

This VOCA program—as described in a January 1989 Des Moines *Register* article—even parallels the suggestion made earlier in this chapter that people of various skills from different states be linked up to serve jointly on the same project. The article described an agricultural project in the Ivory Coast. Counterpart farmers from the United States and the Ivory Coast worked together to develop a corn improvement program in nine villages. Six of the volunteers came from four different Iowa towns, and two were from Minnesota. Each had a specific role, varying from vocational teachers of agricultural to cooperative experts. Interestingly—and again not inconsistent with my projections on developing and expanding such a world development organization—two of these volunteers were ex–Peace Corps workers who wanted to repeat their original experience on a short-term basis, and had specific cultural experience. The primary organizational problem seems to have been that the team did not have an interpreter for the first couple of weeks. In the future, instant translators will resolve that problem.

Certainly, such a volunteer approach—supported by the government when it comes to transportation and per diems—is commendable, and one can only hope that innovative legislation will expand such efforts. But there are still a few words of caution to be given. We don't know what bureaucratic controls are involved in the program. While the VOCA legislation was enacted in 1954, no money was made available until the 1985 farm bill, "when Representative Bereuter wrote an amendment calling for one-tenth of one percent of U.S. foreign aid to be used for the farmer-to-farmer program" part of the bill.[11] After having been in effect for two years, only 46 projects were carried out in 1987. Foreign aid is running at about $26 billion, so 0.1 percent would mean an annual budget of about $130 million. Given that VOCA volunteers receive no salary, there must be a lot of money going to bureaucratic expenses. The logistical expenses of 46 projects just don't add up to that much. What would happen if that $130 million were unleashed on a volunteer world-development organization with no bureaucratic overhead expenses because its administrators and coordinators would also be volunteers? The answer is that a great deal more that 46 projects would happen. We must be ever vigilant when government bureaucracies get their hands on a good idea. The overhead can too easily waste resources and diminish the program's effectiveness.

However, the VOCA program should not be discredited. Its underlying philosophy may be a bit arrogant and naive: Representative Bereuter supposedly got the idea for the program on a trip abroad when he became convinced "that all they need in some of these countries is a couple of Nebraska farmers to show how to get things done." But it is a creative approach that, with a totally volunteer management, would lead to a much higher cost/benefit payoff. I provide the address of the program for those who have never heard of it before.

Volunteers in Overseas Cooperative Assistance (VOCA)
50 F Street, N.W.
Suite 1075
Washington, D. C. 20001
telephone: (202) 620– 8750

## HOW THE END OF THE COLD WAR CAN HELP

It was during the same conference in Omaha at which Bleakely of the State Department spoke that Oleg Derkousky of the Soviet embassy also presented his remarks (see Chapter 2). Derkousky focused on the apparent recognition by the Soviet state that its future international role must be to find ways by which it can work *together* with the West in developing Third World countries, rather than continuing to serve as a technical resource for regional and international conflict. The resources spent for destruction—Derkousky said—would be better spent on construction and the production of a more equitable and just global economic system.[12]

What a revelation! Within the context of our perspective on the Soviet Union's international posture over the past thirty years, this just couldn't happen. Oh, how we want to believe it is really true. And oh, how, we equally want to believe that our own government will reanalyze its world outlook, and start making policy changes in the way it behaves with the rest of the world. Who would have thought that such a fortuitous change in the international climate could occur at the end of the Reagan administration?

As of 1989 (and hopefully I won't have to make last-minute revisions due to the Soviet premier's having been deposed and the Cold War icing up again), all the evidence indicates that the Soviets are following through with their new policies. The Afghanistan pullback really did occur; Angola was resolved; the Sandinistas in Nicaragua are to receive no more Soviet weapons until their human rights record improves; and the screws are being tightened on Fidel Castro's international adventures. We can only hope that all this will continue.

And if it does continue, what could that mean for a bona fide world-development effort? If Derkousky's statements are an accurate representation of policy, it could mean a great deal. Paralleling the logistical arrangements with the U.S. military already suggested, volunteer coordinators might be able to link up with the Soviet Air Force and Navy for transport. And certainly the Soviets are just as stocked with surplus machinery that could be suitable for development projects. Then too, and again complementing the proposed Western support, Soviet embassy compounds throughout the world could be a bivouac site for volunteer workers on short-term assignments. This would be a tremendous gesture of cooperation, for—after transportation—housing is the second most costly expense for the volunteer workers.

Therefore, such gestures are of primary significance to a sustained cooling of the Cold War. If the two sides can coordinate their efforts and help control the major volunteering expenses of transportation and housing through what is for them a fixed overhead cost (that is, the existing embassy compounds and military flights), then there would be many thousands of people willing to offer their skills to world development projects on a short-term basis. This is already happening in the case of the church volunteers I have discussed, and it can easily be expanded once these two costs are controlled.

So ultimately, Gorbachev's democratic policies may help us create interfaces between the institutional bureaucracies and volunteer efforts to affect a world development. Judging by what is already happening in the way of expanded civilian/government interaction—as described earlier—this is a possibility whose time has arrived. Such a proposal ten years ago would have in fact been a dream. But today, it could very well come true.

## A FINAL WORD ON COORDINATION

Throughout this chapter I have stressed the need for coordination, without which the various telecommunications opportunities and logistical resources would never come together. Ten years ago a way of handling this coordination through volunteers did not exist. But today the situation has changed. This is partly a consequence of the increased militancy of the 13,000 returned Peace Corps volunteers, who now constitute a significant body of international development specialists. It also has something to do with cyclical change: The Yuppie years are in remission, and a "kinder, more gentle" concern for global justice is slowly coming back. This now makes it realistic to imagine a volunteer body taking charge of the coordinating function. Combined with communications technology it can spearhead a world development.

In the fall of 1986, I attended the twenty-fifth anniversary celebration of the Peace Corps, held in Washington, D.C. The one concern repeated in all the speeches had to do with how this large body of highly specialized and experienced people could be put to use leading world-development efforts, after their formal service was completed. Out of that gathering came a strengthening of what was then a very struggling organization: the (NCRPCV).[13] Subsequently, the NCRPCV's membership rose to 13,000, and it continues to rise. The NCRPCV, however, is not controlled by the Corps; and although the council of returned volunteers approves of collaborative relationships with Washington, it marches to its own drummer.

On the other hand, the NCRPCV does look like the most viable candidate to pioneer the project of world-development coordination, and develop prototype mechanisms. This is especially so in view of the fact that its membership is projected to rise to more than 100,000 in the next decade. This organization is a large corps of specialists who have already internalized a global development view. Moreover, each of them already has very specific experience in what it means to try to develop—to help— other cultures and other people. NCRPCV members have already been trained in the organizational aspects of getting people involved in technology change, of organizing people to work jointly, and of working with the various traditional institutions that can serve as resources—and all for the purpose of creating and sustaining a world development. Its members are mostly professionals; they are reasonably affluent, but have still retained their original ideology and are now in a position—both economically and professionally—to continue what they started as young men and women. Harnessing that kind of diverse skill, singular commitment, and forceful capacity within a volunteer development organization can be extremely effective—for the NCRPCV membership includes, congressmen, lawyers, doctors, and even commercial advertisers. (Where do you think those Peace Corps ads—"The Toughest Job You'll Ever Love"—come from?)

With a little bit of luck, then, NCRPCV will probably be the first vehicle for setting up a large-scale, integrated volunteer pathway to a new world. It certainly has all the attributes that such an organization will need. But capable ex-volunteers alone cannot do the job. To sustain the first efforts, we will ultimately need a citizenry that understands the importance of creating a new world. Educating our children to that understanding will be the subject of Chapter 7.

## NOTES

1. Author's notes from a rice irrigation project, Guinea-Bissau, 1982.
2. *VITA Newsletter*, February 1985.
3. Information obtained from an interview with faculty in the Department of Communications, University of Northern Iowa, September 8, 1987.
4. A description of the potential quality and applications of high definition television was presented on the *CBS Evening News*, January 10, 1989.
5. Joseph Campbell, *The Power of Myth* (New York: Doubleday, 1988).
6. Ibid.
7. Bleakley K., Address to the Ninth Annual Third World Conference, Omaha, Nebraska, October 1988.
8. *National Council of Returned Peace Corps Volunteers Newsletter*, December 1988, pp. 2–3.
9. Author's notes from a conversation with an NCRPCV volunteer bureaucrat on January 18, 1989.
10. Des Moines *Register*, Agribusiness section, January 15, 1989, p. J-2.
11. Ibid.

12. Oleg Derkousky, Address to the Ninth Annual Third World Conference, Omaha, Nebraska, October 1988.

13. Author's notes of a speech given by Sargent Shriver, Twenty-fifth Anniversary Celebration of Peace Corps, Washington, D.C., September 1986.

# SEVEN

# Education and World Development

In a society such as the United States—where there exists no consistent mythology or beliefs about one's role in one's own society and the world—we may be producing a generation of people who have no real cultural guidelines to restrain them in either their juvenile or adult behavior. For some, this makes no real difference and may in fact even be helpful in their search for truth. Not having a heavy load of cultural beliefs imposed on them, they don't have to spend much energy dumping it when they discover its limitations. However, for the majority, such a beliefless upbringing allows them the freedom only to create their own distorted values and ideas about who they are and how they should act. As Joseph Campbell says, the results are all around us, especially in the cities: What remains of our declining total number of juveniles becomes even more entrenched or entranced with drug usage, and their gang warfare exhibits a standard of brutality that shows how little conventional conduct these children have ever seen.[1]

Lacking any consistent beliefs, moral behavior, or code of conduct has hurt us as a nation. The Japanese, for example, do not have this problem. They still know (believe) that they are God's children and that there is a unique purpose to their being on this planet. The dominance and control of the family by the mothers (Japanese fathers turn over their paychecks to their wives and are given an allowance established by them) further assures that Japanese children grow up knowing who they are and firmly subscribing to a national cultural view that they have internalized as a process of this upbringing. The reason you don't see anarchy on Japanese streets is because Japanese mothers wouldn't stand for it. That may sound simplistic, but it's also basically true.

Given that—which is largely the case—home in the United States is no longer the place to pick up beliefs and values, and that for most children the church has even less effect, what institution in our society can perform that function? As the reader can already guess from my earlier indications, it is the educational system. And that system is fraught with its own problems, stemming from the depressing history of states' rights and isolationism that have ruled it from the start.

Still, the modern necessity of two-earner families (now more than 60 percent of all families), and the basic lack of attention to the upbringing of our children, are bound to increase as we enter the next millennium. The school system has become the only institution where most children can be affected by adults, when it comes to developing values and beliefs. Therefore, it is the one environment where the majority of our children could acquire the beliefs and values that would make them see themselves as members of a global community with an obligation to help others.

Campbell, too, expressed this concern about producing people who will view themselves as members of a global society.

All this hope for something happening in society has to count for something in the human psyche, a whole new way of experiencing a society. And the crucial question here, as I see it, is simply: with what society, what social group, do you identify yourself? Is it going to be with all the planet, or is it going to be with your own particular ingroup? . . . Why can't something of that kind take place in the world right now? [2]

I would add to Campbell's finely stated view that the "whole new way of experiencing a society" must be aggressively pursued if we are to produce people who identify with the planet. Fortunately, we can be fostering that "something in the human psyche" right now, with the behavioral technology already at our disposal. If we appeal to the underlying physiological need to help one another that is in us all (see Chapter 1)—which for many of us has to be unfrozen from the constraints of cultural conditioning that restrict it to our own particular in-group—then there is a chance we can change the existing world view of our children. I'm not saying this is going to be easy. In effect, we will have to reexamine how the dominant-nation stance that for forty years—since the end of World War II—too many of us have regarded as our just rewards of manifest destiny. Recent circumstances such as the war in Vietnam, the corruption in high places of our government, and the success of the more democratic industrial practices we see in Japan and Germany have substantially affected that manifest destiny and our fit within the global order. If we are to play a role in world development that goes beyond nineteenth-century gunboat diplomacy, then we will have to find a way to do some switching—some redirecting—within the inner psyche that motivates our outward behavior.

In olden days of not so long ago, the institution that partway played a role in this was the church. And as Campbell says, ideally the church would have directed that people "must live not in terms of their own ego system, their own devices, but in terms of what you might call the sense of mankind—the christ-in-you."[3]

But religion, in the United States at least, failed in this capacity. My own childhood experience is similar to that of many others: Instruction by the church was largely limited to showing us children that, though other religion's practices may be right spirited, they're in the wrong ballpark. We were not to treat members of other cultures and religions unkindly, but were always to remember—nevertheless—that ours was the one blessed by God. It was the only one on the right track.

Where my experience is dissimilar, however, is that during my early adolescent years the minister of the Methodist church that my family attended was basically a secular humanist. His sermons were redolent with the beauty and wonder of all cultures and the need to serve all mankind. The local Catholic priest was his buddy; our Sunday schools exchanged classes, the priest would give sermons in our church, and so on. The minister taught us that heaven and hell are what we produce on earth— not necessarily something encountered after death. In short order, the church elders got tired of him and brought a Bible thumper into town, instead—(which led quickly to my lack of interest in attending church services.) But the teaching of that man certainly helped shape my world view into that of believing we must yield some of our own benefits to all living beings.

Ministers like this one have been too few and far between, and one could argue that finding school teachers who set such an example is even more difficult. But since religion can't do it (and more than half of all U.S. families aren't active in religion, anyway), the public school system is what we have to work with. It is the only institution (other than television) that has a pervasive, long-term effect on our young people, and we will have to utilize it wisely if we are to influence the psyches of our young nation's children. An effort will be made in this chapter to show how that can be done. One tool at our disposal in changing human behavior is operant conditioning—a tool that is still somewhat controversial.

## WHAT IS OPERANT CONDITIONING?

Operant conditioning is a behavioral tool that is as old as the human species (for everyone uses it intuitively), yet is often feared and denigrated because so many people associate it with nefarious possibilities such as the control and brainwashing of unwilling or unknowing victims. Certainly the decades of the Cold War have had something to do with this notion, for the so-called brainwashing of U.S. POWs during the Korean War was a form of operant conditioning. But if one would denigrate operant conditioning as being evil, then one must accuse motherhood of the same—for every effective mother, in fact, uses operant conditioning.

In its simplest practice, operant conditioning is the reinforcing of a certain behavior by rewarding it. As B. F. Skinner states, "Behavior is shaped and maintained by its [reward] consequences." [4] The reward may be verbal, monetary, or otherwise substantive. The odds are very high that, following the reinforcement period, the individual will continue to repeat that behavior in the future. Consequently, to get a person to behave or believe in a certain way, one need only devise a set of rewards that will reinforce that particular behavior.

For example, take the classic case of a mother wanting her child to pick up his clothes. In accordance with the theory, she should reinforce the proper behavior on the spot, when it is done. Therefore, when the mother sees her child actually picking up his clothes, after he finishes she immediately praises him for doing so. If she knows there is something that he particularly wants—such as a cookie—she might also give the child a cookie. The mother has then reinforced the child with both a verbal and a substantive reward. The odds are that the child will repeat the behavior: He will pick up his clothes again. And because research shows that intermittent rather than continuous reinforcement produces the biggest change, the mother shouldn't reward the child if he picks up his clothes the next day, but wait a couple of days before again reinforcing the behavior.

The rationale for intermittent versus continuous is that continuous reinforcement becomes expected as part of the daily routine, and loses its effect as a reinforcer. The intermittent reinforcer keeps the mind guessing—not complacent—knowing subconsciously that one has to continue a certain behavior to get its reward once in a while. Over time, the new behavior becomes integrated into one's total behavior and the reinforcers—intermittent or continuous—are no longer needed or will only have to be occasionally refreshed if the desired behavior weakens.

Everybody recognizes the scenario I have described. They've done it with their own kids (with varying degrees of success); their mothers did it with them (with varying degrees of success). And all cultures use the same behavioral mechanism.

But let's modify the scenario a bit. Say Johnny is now sixteen and starting to play with a group of devil worshipers. His friends take him to an isolated retreat and bombard him with devil worship stimuli. As he exhibits behavior supportive of devil worship, his colleagues reward him on his progress. Being a teenager in the late twentieth century, these rewards could be drugs or sex with a coven mate. In this setting, sex and drugs will be as effective as verbal praise and cookies. The odds are that, after a few weeks of this, the world will have another committed devil worshiper. This is, in effect, what happened to Patty Hearst when she was held captive by the Symbionese Liberation Army and ultimately joined them.

Like any powerful technology, then, operant conditioning has the capacity for either evil or good. We must assume that, in a properly designed program with all the monitoring mechanisms in place—such as public disclosure and involvement of parents, in the case of school-sponsored conditioning programs—good will prevail. Certainly—given recent disclosures of, for example, drug parties and sales by employees in some New York City schools—we would not want to sanction such behavioral powers without monitoring what is going on. Grass-roots control and participation of all the players is essential.

## GLOBAL AWARENESS IN THE CLASSROOM

To effect a concern in our children for a volunteer-directed world development, we have to go further than reinforcing them with cookies. The schools must be directed to condition them systematically to behave in a globally concerned manner. It's also important to point out that some school systems and teachers already do this, intuitively and overtly. For example, let's consider what may have prompted a group of New York City children to respond as they did to the 1986 famine in Ethiopia.[5]

Apparently, this particular high school class had a social studies teacher who wanted to get across the moral problems involved with living in a reasonably comfortable First World while a substantial number of fellow human beings live in dire poverty. (Such is the world that C. P. Snow envisioned in the late 1950s— a world where citizens of the developed countries watch mass starvation on their color TV sets while they eat dinner.) Perhaps during the process of group discussion, it was suggested to the class members that they didn't have to sit idle by the wayside and watch the problem go down. They could in fact do something about it.

And do something they did. In the end, the students collected enough money to buy a planeload of grain and ship it to

Ethiopia—and in a much faster time than the professional bureaucratic organizations were able to. It seems to me that their teacher must have been using a great deal of verbal reinforcement as the students carried out this project, and the final reinforcement came with all the national acclaim that the students received. Their achievement confirms not only my view that we can change people's behavior, but also that volunteer efforts—because the primary motivation is to serve, not to perpetuate a bureaucratic institution—can be more effective in organizing and implementing solutions to human needs than the professional organizations are. This example proves that even children can be more effective than professional bureaucrats.

Thinking about the teacher who led this project brings up a critical issue. Any world-development conditioning program in the schools will only be as good as the teachers who carry it out. If the teachers do not understand the process and do not carry it out in an intelligent, systematic, and consistent manner, then it will either not work at all or only have marginal results.

One way of enlisting the teachers and ensuring their effectiveness is through retrofit workshops. First off, the objectives of producing the world-development generation would have to be worked through all levels of the school system, getting conceptual and operational input from all the teachers. Again, there are organizational and behavioral reasons why this input is necessary, as discussed in Chapter 4. In essence, the reason is commitment. Without involvement and the right to participate, there will be no commitment. And there can be no enduring program in the schools without commitment on the part of the teachers, especially if the school administrators simply dictate such a program—as they are wont to do. A recent survey shows a predominant dissatisfaction among teachers with their lack of involvement in the design of curriculum.[6] Not involving teachers in the design of an intensive behavior-change program would spell disaster.

Thus, there is a basic dilemma in creating a global-concern curriculum, for the change will generally only occur if the catalyst of a local school board or school administrator is in there deciding that it should be done, and then following through and making sure that it happens. Accordingly, the impetus to get such programs going may, in the end, be federal. Just as in the 1960s the Kennedy and Johnson administrations pushed laws through that finally ensured the civil liberties of all citizens of this country—most particularly, its black citizens—and led to racial integration of the school systems in every state, so too it may be necessary to produce federal legislation requiring school boards to guarantee that a concern for and involvement with global development become a key component of student education.

Now I'm not saying that governors will be standing in front of schoolhouse doors (as George Wallace of Alabama did in the 1960s) to prevent the introduction of such a curriculum and I certainly don't expect that the National Guard will have to be called in, but I do anticipate some local resistance to such a program and particularly to the method (operant conditioning) of getting it across. There are certain things that the federal government could do to sweeten the process, without creating another bureaucratic quagmire. Why not develop (using President Bush's "1,000 lights" promotion of volunteerism) a creative combination of federal and volunteer efforts to coordinate and manage such an educational campaign among our children? As mentioned in Chapter 6, it's already being done to a certain extent by the NCRPCV through Biden-Pell grants and volunteer contributions, but we need to go further than that. Limited federal support could be very useful in this regard.

Instead of having a bureaucracy-imposed curriculum, it would make more sense to utilize a combined design-team effort. That is, certainly a federal design outline could be contracted and disseminated to all the state education agencies. But it would be purposely provided with the recognition that schools must have the freedom to modify the plan, and that organizations such as the NCRPCV may interact with it (without losing federal support funds).

For example, the federal manual could include an exercise showing students how international economic systems adversely affect Third World countries, and it might be written as presented below.

*Objective*: To show students how First World economic systems work to the disadvantage of Third World countries.

*Possible Methods of Getting That Idea Across*:

• Do a role play in which one group of students plays the part of copper producers in Chile, and another group plays the part of copper buyers in the United States.

1. The students in the first group are instructed as to the kind of technology they have to use, what their total costs are, and consequently the price they must charge to make a profit.

2. The students in the second group know that, with the development of fiber optics, they can now demand a lower price. They are instructed to insist on a price lower than the copper producers' asking price. And the buyers get what they want.

• After the role play, discuss what took place, including the following items in your discussion:

1. What happened to the laborers when the production company couldn't make a profit?

2. Is it right for one country to dominate another country so much, in terms of its economic production system?

3. Are there ways in which an equitable price could be determined so that everyone profits reasonably?

4. Is the process depicted in this role play one that it is conducive to creating a fair and equitable global community?

Of course, the teacher presiding over all this should be trained in conditioning techniques. Whenever a student makes a response appropriate to the objectives of the exercise or goes even further than expected in terms of understanding and sensitivity to the issues, then the teacher reinforces that response with a verbal conditioner. A system of formal recognition rewards could also be developed that would even further reinforce appropriate behaviors.[7]

The main point here, however, is that this is a possible example from a manual of federal guidelines: It would serve only as a prototype, which the school would be free to use as is or modify. Properly trained teachers would fill in the details and modify the exercise to match the nature of their classes. And jointly selected monitors from volunteer organizations would review the modifications to assure federal officials that global

concerns were continuing to be addressed. An even more specific curriculum example will be presented later in the chapter.

One strategy that could be used to alleviate resistance to such
a process of instruction is to involve parents and teachers in
oversight committees—thus making sure that all parents have
the opportunity to understand what is happening, what the
program's objectives are, and what can be expected in terms of
a better global society. Above all, the idea is to eliminate any
fears that a plot to brainwash their children for some evil purpose
is taking place. This involvement of parent/teacher oversight
committees is something that should be taking place, anyway,
in all aspects of school administration. A school system that
doesn't involve the parents is very likely a school system that
does not serve its charges well. I've already alluded to the New
York City school system where some employees allegedly
"sponsored" after-hours drug parties on school grounds.

Now the next trick is to make such an educational system
work without producing another federal bureaucracy and without having to pay much for it. Here again, volunteer development organizations can come into play. The volunteer
organization would administer the training of teachers, development of curriculum, coordination of state and federal resources, and implementation of materials. This would cut costs
and eliminate federal control. Ideally, the volunteer operators
should be a mix of parents, teachers, and local citizens who have
expertise and interest in the subject matter. In one program
already being executed, a chapter of the NCRPCV in Northern
California—using a Biden-Pell grant to cover travel expenses—
is helping to design a global awareness project in the schools.
They visit classes and talk to students about their Peace Corps
experiences, and discuss ways in which a more just world can
be created.[8]

Retired people can also play a pivotal role in any volunteer-
monitored educational system because—for one thing—they are
readily available, but mostly because they have a world experience that often expands and personalizes the history that the
students are studying. (For example, there are some people alive
who were actually in the great San Francisco earthquake of 1906;
there are many more who fought in World War I; and so on.

What better way to study the twentieth century than to hear the perceptions of a person who has lived it.) Let's consider for a moment the scale of the volunteer resource we are talking about. In my own county in Iowa (with a total county population of about 120,000), there are 1,200 senior citizens working in such groups as the federally sponsored Retired Senior Volunteer Program (RSVP), with skills that range from university teaching to corporate management to farming. These people are alert, active, and willing to involve themselves in any reasonable endeavor that is satisfying to them and helps promote their community and state. They constitute a resource that is available and expanding in size throughout the country; it should not be wasted, especially when all we need is a little logistical support money to mobilize its forces.

Certainly, in the case of administrating a volunteer school program, senior citizens could perform that function working either out of somebody's living room or in a spare room at the school. And the beauty of it all is that the program will be getting high-quality labor at a magnificent price: nothing. The seniors themselves may get a boost from their volunteer activities. Studies associate the involvement and commitment of volunteering with health benefits that can even prolong life (see Chapter 1).

In any case, all such volunteer approaches are consistent with the one myth that we do have about the Great American Society: that we are a nation of people that helps those who are in need. True, we may have strayed somewhat during the self-centered years of the 1980s. But as I began organizing for a project in my own home communities a couple of years ago, I kept hearing local people repeatedly state a desire to be helping others, to find some way to play a volunteer part in making other peoples' lives better. And this wasn't just in Iowa—often viewed as deviant because of its "goodness rating"—but also in my second home in Southern California, which is considered by many people to be the very seat of selfishness. There seems to be a need among a sizeable number of our citizens to be involved in helping others, and there is no reason why they cannot help create a new educational system that will instill the global-concern values our children will need in the upcoming millenium.

## CREATING THE NEXT GENERATION

One must understand the underlying psychological basis behind behavioral change efforts. B. F. Skinner in his book *Beyond Freedom and Dignity* has this to say:

The literature of freedom has encouraged escape from . . . all control. . . . Control is clearly the opposite of freedom, and if freedom is good, control must be bad. What is overlooked is control which does not have adverse consequences at any time. . . . Many social practices essential to the welfare of the species involve the control of one person by another, and without them a society is in trouble.[9]

Once again, we see that mothers have always had this understanding: It is they who largely condition children, and control them in the early years.

Skinner argues that it is necessary "not to free men from control but to analyze and change the kinds of control to which they are exposed."[10] Creating a generation to carry out a world development will certainly involve Skinner's variety of benevolent control, for "without help a person acquires very little moral or ethical behavior under either natural or social contingencies. . . . Education imparts rules which make it possible to satisfy both natural and social contingencies without being directly exposed to them."[11]

As noted earlier, education in late twentieth-century societies has had to replace the moral and ethical conditions that too often are no longer provided by the family or church. The irony is that, even as this need for control in the schools becomes more compelling, the nation's quest for greater individual freedom restricts its application. Yet if we want to design the new cultures of the twenty-first century—and given that the trend is toward the family exercising even less moral control—then the educational system will have to take the bull by the horns and be responsible for developing a curriculum and an environment that can produce adults with the internalized global concerns to live in that new world about which this present generation can only imagine.

What specifically will we have to do to create the behavior

and attitudes needed for a kinder and gentler nation that will become integrated into a global community? The process would have to be a dynamic one, and implemented at all levels of education from kindergarten through twelfth grade. It would no doubt require a modification of the current school curriculum, as well as retraining of the current fleet of instructors. That is, two years of special instruction in elementary school and one year in high school just won't do the job. All levels must complement each other, and be integrated throughout the curriculum. Additionally, the kind of conditioners must be adjusted to the level of education: What works in elementary school classrooms cannot be expected to work in high school classrooms. An effective global awareness program would be much more extensive than the conducting of isolated exercises such as was described earlier in the chapter.

Consider the case of the elementary classroom: How would one go about showing very young students that they fit within a larger world dynamic, and get them to assimilate the value of helping others who may not be so fortunate as they? At the early elementary level where the cognitive skills ain't so great, physical involvement seems to be the answer. Hence the reliance in the California progressive education system of the early 1950s on building projects to illustrate concepts, which has the additional advantage of teaching children to work effectively in small groups—a skill important to their working in international development teams later in life. Building some of the physical artifacts of a different culture allows the elementary school student both to become aware of differences and to be rewarded (conditioned) for her or his acceptance and understanding of that culture. It is to be expected that this process will affect the student's long-term attitude toward and understanding of a globally integrated world. Let me be more specific with an example of how this could be carried out in a third-grade classroom:

*Objective*: To engender an understanding of Bolivian culture and to impart a belief in the student that citizens of the country studied are as entitled to an economically secure life as the student is.

At the third-grade level, reading assignments combined with lecture and discussion cannot be as effective as they might be in high school. Remember that we as adults are able to develop a reasonably understanding of, say, adobe by reading about its physical characteristics and its uses. However, third-graders need to muck in it; and that is exactly what they should do. Make a batch of adobe—three parts clay; one part straw—and add water to mix it up; mold it, and let it dry. Do all that, and you have a better than reasonable understanding of what the stuff is and what you can do with it as a building material, as well as what it's like to live in a house built of it.

*Synthesis*: Okay, now that everybody has experienced adobe, what are some of it's advantages and disadvantages?

*Responses*:

1. It smells musty, and it dissolves when you put water on it.

2. It's dirty; mud gets on you when you brush alongside it.

*Evaluation*: What does it mean to people who have no choice but to live in houses made of this material?

• Are they worse off than us because of it?

• Above all, are there reasons why people must live in dwellings of this nature?

This final question then sets the stage for the ultimate purpose in doing all this stuff: to give the student some hands-on knowledge of how differently people of the Third World live, and an intimate realization of what makes that environment different from our culture. This provides a chance for the teacher to reward responses that are supportive of global understanding. How? Suppose in the course of discussion the students ask why it is necessary for most Bolivians to live under such conditions. The teacher would then explain how economic systems affect the distribution of wealth. At some point, one or more students may come up with the suggestion that it is the responsibility of the richer countries to see that all people of the world share in the global wealth. This is the precise point at which the teacher may verbally reinforce the student's interpretation of what has been presented. If—as explained earlier—the reinforcement is given more randomly than consistently, the odds are that it will lead to further curiosity on the part of all the students, and may even inspire a plan of action. I imagine that the New York teacher whose class organized that airlift of food to Ethopia must have done something analogous during class discussions that changed those students' beliefs and behavior.

Thus, we see the importance of the instructor in this process. A mother who is working to reinforce behaviors appropriate for the functioning of the household must be persistent and constantly monitor her children's progress. This is no less so for the teacher, and is the reason why teachers who have not already gone through some training in the development, use, and monitoring of operant technique will need to do so.

Utilizing a well-developed curriculum with coordinated followup throughout a student's development, then, the educational system can reinforce behaviors and develop values conducive to a new world development. As Skinner says, "We change the way a person looks at something, as well as what he sees when he looks, by changing the contingencies."[12] If we believe that a concern for world development is important, then we can shape how our students look at the outside world in support of that view by positively rewarding the suitable behavior. The chances are that they will internalize that concern as their own.

## FINAL COMMENTS ON THE USE OF CONDITIONING TECHNIQUES

In the case of very young students such as in the Head Start program, a highly effective reinforcer is food. Students do their assignments well and they get a cracker. But as students get older, the reinforcers must become more sophisticated and subtle. They are more often verbal then, and depend on the persuasive abilities of the teachers who are carrying out the reinforcement. We must never forget the importance of that role. When the teacher verbally shows a caring attentiveness, she or he reinforces whatever behavior the student has just emitted. That caring function, of course, applies to all forms of learning in kindergarten through twelfth grade—not just the world-development component.

School systems need to develop in teachers a better awareness of their important role in reinforcing behavior, and encourage them to focus their attentiveness on behaviors that have a re-deeming global—that is, social justice—value. Unfortunately, operant conditioning seems to be largely ignored in the curric-ulum for teachers (according to professors in my university's school of education).[13] Some administrators even view the tech-nique as too radical.

But operant conditioning is not a radical technique, and its application in creating global concerns already exists to some extent. I mentioned earlier the New York class where students developed their own Ethiopian relief program. There are also historical examples. My own elementary school education is a case in point. In the late 1940s and early 1950s, the progressive education system—which employed experiential learning and operant conditioning—was the primary vehicle of elementary education in California, and I was one of its lucky recipients. Elementary school classrooms were designed to have additional space for constructing class projects, as well as a series of work-benches equipped with carpentry tools and materials. When we studied airplane technology—for instance—we not only read about it but also (both girls and boys) constructed planes, ac-cording to our individual interest and design. And when we studied other cultures, we would likewise totally immerse our-selves into it. The third-grade adobe curriculum that I presented earlier in the chapter is based on one of the projects we did in my own third-grade class. And—consonant with the techniques of operant conditioning—whenever any one of us did particu-larly outstanding work on a project, she or he would receive a reward of additional independent time in the "carpentry shop" (but no food rewards). Our understanding of differences in the world—of life beyond Southern California—was consequently reinforced by our hands-on learning and by the rewards we received for behaving with some awareness of that other world.

Another important input in my case—and this was indepen-dent of the objectives of progressive education—was that several of our teachers had relocated to our school system after teaching during World War II at the Japanese-American citizen concen-tration camp at Manzanar, California (about 60 miles from my hometown). These teachers conditioned us with an awareness born of their experience. Thus, at an early age we internalized an understanding of the fragility of constitutional government and a sense of the injustices that often occur to people who are physically different—that is, minorities.

I believe that these early childhood experiences of mine—even though they were not so coordinated and concentrated as we now need in order to instill the next generation with a concern about world development—were largely responsible for my later decision to work in the field of international development. And what is significant here is that I got this awareness specifically from the school system (supported later by our Methodist minister in California), for global development concerns were not a particular interest with my parents.

In a world whose people must quickly teach themselves how to understand and support each other for mutual survival, how can teaching colleges and school systems possibly object to an educational process that will promote a global concern among students? One state—California—has used it in the recent past and with salubrious effect, I'd say. There is no technical reason why all states cannot now do so—no reason why conditioning technology cannot be applied to making the behavior and values of our children more compassionate and globally inclusive.

## THE DESIGN OF THE GLOBAL AWARENESS CULTURE

In *Beyond Freedom and Dignity*, Skinner explains the evolution of a culture as a series of contingency reinforcers.[14] The reinforcers in a strong culture produce citizens who are quite willing to die voluntarily for their country in the quest for a higher order. Or as Joseph Campbell would say, they possess a willingness to die for their country's myths.

The numerous contingency reinforcers in Nazi Germany—Hitler youth; a national scapegoat for frustrations in the person of the Jews (which was basically a newly orchestrated version of an old cruelty toward the underclass and its achievements, since pogroms ever since the days of the Romans had long since compromised the genetic purity of the Jewish race in Europe);

and government subsidies in the form of jobs, grants to large families, and a national health plan—made it possible for Adolf Hitler to sacrifice a whole generation of Germans to a cause that other cultures knew was evil. This sort of thing is the reason why people fear conditioning programs. But we are not Depression-era Germans, and we don't have a totalitarian government. There is little reason to believe that a coordinated operant-conditioning program would produce a Nazi America.

In fact, the lack of sufficient cultural-contingency reinforcers probably explains some of the failings in our present generation of young people. If we can believe the studies and editorials we read, then the two-earner family does not have the time to provide the reinforcers that once helped young people to establish a relationship with the greater entity: their culture. Even if in the past that process was based on myth (that is, the United States as keeper of democracy for the world), at least it provided a philosophical base for the nation's youth. This was a spiritual beacon that either would continue to be believed in adulthood or else would be debunked as the person became educated and experienced. We have lacked such a beacon in our time, especially since the Vietnam War.

For too many families today, the predominant cultural reinforcer is the television set. And as a reinforcer, especially in the 1970s and 1980s, it supported a very dangerous set of behaviors. The drug culture was glamorized; violence and aggressiveness were presented as a way of life; and the acceptance of these "cultural norms" was further tightened by the use of very sophisticated and pleasing commercials. With that as the predominant vehicle for conditioning—and with minimal parent interaction—is it any wonder that this generation of young people has problems? And if we can blame anyone for the mess, it's not the dopeheads of the 1960s—who are only now in their forties, and have not been making the decisions that have laid this trip on the nation—but the old fogies (whatever their age) who still retain a nineteenth-century view of economics: Use anything—regardless of the social cost—that will maximize profits. Skinner maintains that "a culture which for any reason induces its members to work for its survival is more likely to survive."[15] It is seriously open to question whether the culture of United States has carried out this basic survival function with the present generation.

In any case, if the United States cannot get its act together in the training of its young people, then it may very well not be the leader of a new world development. Certainly, other cultures such as the Northern Europeans and the Japanese are doing a better job at this time in educating their children in that direction.

But even if only a small minority of Americans becomes involved with a volunteer world development, we could still have a pioneering effect. That minority could amount to millions of people even if only 15 percent of our population were to accept a global development viewpoint. In other words, maybe it isn't really necessary to affect all the people in the beginning, to mobilize a new world development. Maybe school systems should maximize their effort in this direction by working with the number of children that is likely to produce that 15 percent of adults—and forget the rest, for the moment. Operationally, the global development curriculum might be offered universally at the elementary level, and then the schools would select certain students and direct them to the classes and teachers that would continue to develop their global perspective as they go through high school. Consequently, the limited resources of school budgets and qualified faculty could be utilized in such a way that the world would benefit from having at least "a few good" men and women capable of playing a leadership role in world development. In effect, this occurred on a national level in the late 1940s, since only California was using the techniques of progressive education; and it may explain why California led the country in the number of young college graduates who joined the Peace Corps in the 1960s.

This more elitist and concentrated change approach—given the difficulty of acquiring staff and budget money—may be the best way to begin shaping a global awareness culture in the United States. It may well be that affecting all the people at the same time cannot be achieved, but that a target goal of 15 percent of the adult population could be accomplished in one generation. If we do a good job on a few—rather than a bad job on all—we would still be addressing Skinner's concern that we create citizens who will be responsible to a global society, and not just to themselves. We would simply be responding to the question as to how we can go about rapidly producing such a globally oriented citizenry. In the United States, the educational system is the only remaining institutional means to carry out that behavioral change process. Will 15 percent of the school population produce a sufficient base to affect a global concern and new world development? We won't know until we've tried.

## FINAL COMMENTS ON THE GLOBAL CULTURE

Unfortunately, we cannot wait around for a world-development culture to evolve. We don't have a few hundred years. We have to design and create that culture as rapidly as possible. From a behavioral viewpoint, Skinner has shown that a child becomes a member of a specific culture through the use of operant conditioning applied by her or his parents and other authority figures within the immediate environment.[16] In terms of creating a new generation whose internalized or acculturated values are conducive to supporting and interfacing with a world development, the trick is to design a cultural mechanism that will produce that kind of person.

Skinner says, "The social contingencies, or the behavior they generate, are the idea of a culture; the reinforcers that appear in the contingencies are its values."[17] These values are then used by the adult members of a culture to reinforce the behavior of its children. The end product is that the next generation accepts and supports the reinforced culture as being good and the way things should be.

To one extent or another, in producing a global culture, all the industrialized societies (who in effect control the world) will need to condition their children to believe that volunteer efforts for a world development are worthwhile for all. And hopefully we'll be able to do better than the 15–percent level of population training suggested earlier.

Apparently, most people do not develop such values on their own. Therefore, society—the governments, the school systems, and hopefully the families—must decide that globally inclusive values are important to our mutual survival and need to be reinforced by specific conditioning tools. The idea is to produce adults who accept those values and in turn inculcate them in their own children. With any luck, this new breed of adults will also help to broaden the base of school training in the generation following them.

Unfortunately, this is one of those beneficial ideas that may wind up being challenged on the basis of the Bill of Rights. It's also likely that an assortment of xenophobic coots would find such a program to be yet another example of "commie" brain-washing. But—as explained in the Skinner quote above—the control or conditioning of specific social values that are of benefit to us as a nation and as a world does not amount to giving up our freedom, but serves as a means to enhance freedom by integrating individual behavior into a world culture. That does not mean that each individual becomes a mindless nonentity controlled by some political force. It means that part of each person's individual behavior is internally controlled so that she or he will be supportive of a new world order in which all cultures and all people are equal. There is no real giving up of personal freedom in all this.

In designing, developing, and implementing such a new culture, it should not be unreasonable to look to the government for financial help. After all, in 1988 we elected an "education president," whose dominant campaign slogan—"1,000 points of light"—ultimately translated to the use of volunteers in solving problems that cannot be handled effectively by bureaucrats. That sounds just fine, particularly if the points of light are kept burning by federal funds. We should be able to expect government support for the volunteer activities of people committed to developing a global culture from our side of the world. But don't hold your breath for that kind of interaction between citizens and their state. Miracles do happen. But most likely, we will have to pull this one off ourselves, and hope that the least we get from the government is minimal harassment.

## CONCLUDING REMARKS

As this chapter has shown, we do already have the behavioral technology to go about creating a generation of adults who live with an internalized belief according to which working for a new world development is an expected way of life. Most certainly, this can be done.

But it has been equally shown that the means of accomplishing this objective is—to say the least—complex, and depends on a variety of resources including the federal and local governments and the aid of parents, teachers, and volunteers. A reliance on state bureaucracies has been shown to be ineffective by both the Soviet and Western models. And if freedom and dignity are to be essential components of our world development, then—as Skinner rightly argues—it is the educational environment that must be changed first. We can change that environment through a combined effort of the resources already mentioned. Most importantly, grass-roots and volunteer organizations must operate the controls of these resources, so that we do not inadvertently create a monstrous world in which people are passively manipulated by a nonparticipative behavioral technology and autonomous state controllers pull the strings.

We have already seen that lack of participation results in failure in the more traditional development ventures throughout the Third World, where programs and projects rise and fall on a regular basis—often creating more harm than good by their transitory character.[18] The ultimate recipients have had no say or input. If the operant reward of these programs should be an improvement in the standard of living, then the conditioner fails because the recipient's desires have not been consulted. To be conditioned, you have to be involved in the process: It can't be done for you.

Both effective operant conditioning and the design of new cultures, then, must include those two essential elements of volunteerism: commitment, and participation. Therefore, if we are seriously talking about a new world development, we must seriously realize that volunteer organizations will have to replace the power of state bureaucracies. The Soviets have shown us that even trying to satisfy basic human needs (food and shelter) by means of nonparticipative, highly controlled, centrally directed bureaucracies doesn't work. In creating a new world of equality and freedom, the very processes of creating that world must be free and open to those who are affected. This applies as much to the Third World person receiving guidance or assistance as it does to the First World children whose values we wish to change.

But there is still one final concern that must be examined here. While we have the technology, and can train people to orient our children toward a new global culture, do we have the will to do so? Unfortunately, in the real world there are many barriers to creating the new one—and that is the subject of the last chapter.

## NOTES

1. J. Campbell, *The Power of Myth* (New York: Doubleday, 1988).

2. Ibid., p. 210.

3. Ibid., p. 211.

4. B. F. Skinner, *Beyond Freedom and Dignity* (New York: Alfred A. Knopf, 1979), p. 128.

5. The reader may remember the television news associated with this story. As well as tell of the children's success in finally getting their shipment of grain freighted off to Ethiopia, the reporting also gave a glimpse of all the media glitter that descended on them.

6. *Chronicle for Higher Education* (May 1987).

7. A book in itself could be written on the specific conditioning systems and rewards that might be developed for a global awareness curriculum. There is not the space to do that within this chapter. However, the reader is referred to the following books by Skinner, which provide more detailed discussions on the kinds of reinforcers that could be used: *Contingencies of Reinforcement* (1969); *The Technology of Teaching* (1968).

8. From the author's conversation with an NCRPCV administrator in the Washington, D.C., office, January 1989.

9. Skinner, *Beyond Freedom and Dignity*, p. 43.

10. Ibid., p. 173.

11. Ibid., p. 173.

12. Ibid., p. 84.

13. I ran a brief survey among professors at the University of Northern Iowa School of Education (which is among the top ten in the country), and discovered that almost nothing about the use of operant conditioning techniques is incorporated into the training of teachers.

14. Skinner, *Beyond Freedom and Dignity*, p. 144.

15. Ibid., p. 145.

16. Ibid., p. 128.
17. Ibid., p. 129.
18. A Jedlicka, *Organizational Change and the Third World* (New York: Praeger, 1987).

# EIGHT

# The Real World: Barriers to Pathfinding a New One

When I began writing this book, volunteerism wasn't very chic. Then the presidential campaigns got underway, and we kept hearing from George Bush about his "1,000 points of light." Finally, after a good deal of public confusion over the term, Bush defined it as comprehensive volunteer work. As president, does he now mean to integrate this into some sort of national plan? We're still not sure what he really meant, and only history will tell us in the end.

Then somewhere around March 1989, Senator Sam Nunn began pushing the idea of national volunteer service in return for college funding. Suddenly volunteerism became fashionable. But because the United States is in an age of control by grandstanding politicians, what was a good idea received a lot of quick national hype (with photo opportunities) and then rapidly died off as other events developed and provided publicity to promote our politician's careers.

But let's examine the idea of national volunteer service. First of all, I'm in favor of at least one year's mandatory national service for all young people (both boys and girls). It wouldn't have to be done in one lump effort; it could be done, say, on weekends and during the summer. But service to their country— whatever the form of service—should be required of all citizens. And—going against all my earlier recommendations here—there would be no democratic participation in the decision to do this. The elder generation would unilaterally impose it on the youth of the nation. How could it be enforced? Well, we wouldn't want to put people in jail for not donating their service, but we could institute a discharge certificate and use that as an enforcer. Without a record of service, you could not get a federal, state, or local government job. And—analogous to a dishonorable military discharge—not having your certificate would complicate your chances of working in the private sector. This would prevent, once again, an enforcement bureaucracy from building up.

No exceptions—neither rich or poor would have any access to exemptions, physical or otherwise (even if destiny should make them a vice-president sometime in the future). Got asthma or flat feet? No problem, there are many community-service jobs that require very little physical effort. And while the rich may still find some way to avoid service, one would hope that such avoidance would have an even more profound effect on a budding political career than, say, National Guard duty during one of the nation's wars. Consequently, the responsibility to serve one's country can easily be imposed on the majority without having to take criminal action, as was done to my generation during the Vietnam War.

Admittedly, such mild coercion may be necessary in the early years of such a program. But it is to be expected that with a new public school curriculum that stresses volunteerism, punishments would gradually become redundant. Young people would believe it their duty to serve their country.

Now, where I differ with others who have proposed schemes for mandatory national service is on the question of who will control the program. I certainly don't want to see the federal government creating another mismanaged bureaucracy.

However—just as for a volunteer world development—there is no reason why the national service system cannot be controlled by the numerous volunteer agencies throughout the country, using the same computer and communications systems I have proposed in earlier chapters. Unfortunately, there would still have to be a small federal bureaucracy to centralize the records of those who have participated; but with volunteers staffing the central office, we could keep it very small indeed.

Operationally, such a wealth of unpaid community-service workers could be absorbed relatively easy. Goodwill might take twenty people; the public school systems, another 100 to serve as tutors; senior citizen organizations, some as go-fers; and hospitals, others as orderlies. There would be no problem in absorbing all those volunteer hours, for in any community there are more than enough volunteer organizations that can use the labor.

So why not get on it right now, and pass the laws that would require young people to give service to their country? The risk of national unrest seems minimal. It is hard to imagine the nation's youth running amuck in the streets at the thought of having to do weekend duty at a nursing home. This is particularly so since—as Abbie Hoffman put it, shortly before he committed suicide—the nation's campuses are a hotbed of social rest. This is not the 1960s. One would expect—based on the numbers of indifferent students we routinely encounter in the universities, and the current acceptance of volunteerism, in general—that riots would not develop, were community service to be made mandatory by law.

Certainly, the pathway to a new world must include integrating more volunteerism into the fabric of our own nation-state. But that subject would fill another book (one that—with all the publicity given to Senator Nunn's ideas—is probably being written by someone else right now). But the subject of this book has been the means by which volunteerism can become an international force for good in developing the world. What the previous chapters have outlined is how that process can be carried out, based on existing technologies. A good way to end is to touch on some current efforts in the real world and to consider—among other things—how they interface with existing Third World governments.

## THE NATURE OF THE HOST GOVERNMENTS

Throughout the 1960s and 1970s it was part of the conventional wisdom to knock the developed world—especially the United States. It became a ritual, both domestic and foreign. And there has been justification for it, too, as our foreign policies have often been notably screwy. One prime example during the 1960s was our sending Peace Corps volunteers to the Third World in the name of peace and international brotherhood while simultaneously destroying other Third World countries such as Vietnam, Laos, and Cambodia.

Knocking the United States was fine in those decades and still may be for those of us who are its citizens. But many of our Third World brothers—particularly diplomats and students—still feel they have the right to do likewise, without acknowledging their own countries' inadequacies. I recall an incident that took place during a conference last year. An Indian expatriate professor was condemning the U.S. political system. Finally, several U.S. professors—myself included—stood up and condemned the Indian political system, particularly its bureaucracy and corruption—which ended in a general screaming match. Damn it, there is nothing worse than one-sided hypocrisy. Most Third World governments greatly exceed our own in stupidity, ignorance, and outright malice toward the majority of their citizens.

Since the 1970s, we have followed the Third World exploits of Emperor Bokassa, who swallowed Jonathan Swift's line and ate babies; Idi Amin, whose execution policy was to drive a spike down the center of his enemy's head; Pol Pot and his genocide in Cambodia; Pinochet and his state terrorism; and General Noriega, who apparently got his jollies by watching the sexual torture of women political prisoners. In other words, the rest of the world ain't so hot. And despite a generalized trend to a sort of democratic behavior throughout much of the world, a good number of Third World governments still aren't very nice at all. What does this mean for volunteer work groups? It means that there must be some discretion and selection exercised in deciding who to work with, for—obviously—development groups in Ankeny, Iowa, don't want to be cooperating with Pol Pot and his people.

This should not really put a damper on the process I have proposed because, for one thing, the demonstration effect of volunteer projects can be contagious, and can promote a more democratic behavior on the part of the host government. This seems to be happening in Nicaragua.

What happened in China during May 1989 stemmed from a somewhat analogous situation. To a large extent, the student rebellion occurred because exchange students who had experienced living in the United States returned home with news of a different world out there. One thing led to another, as they described their experiences to students within China. What ultimately resulted were the street actions we witnessed via satellite TV.

And while, for the time being, that particular quest for freedom has been suppressed, one thing is certain: The Chinese students established a baseline that all oppressed Third World people may well follow. Improved communications and the input of volunteers will help to speed it along.

## THE LIMITATIONS OF THE CONSTITUTION—A CURRICULUM BARRIER

Obviously, the Constitution has been a major determining factor of U.S. government for more than 200 years. And as we all know from our civics classes, it has been the quintessential document historically. Clones of our system were instituted in the other Western countries as the global political system changed from monarchist autocratic control to largely people-controlled systems in the late eighteenth and early nineteenth centuries.

Unfortunately, however, because ours was the first, it had no one else's mistakes to learn from. And while it does have an amendment clause to correct its errors (a very laborious, time-consuming process), the original document failed us in the area of education. It left public education as a state's right, thus ensuring that no uniform standards would be developed and that no rapid means of revising the educational system on a national level could ever occur. This being left in the hands of the states produces a very inconsistent product. For example, in my hometown in Iowa, we have an outstanding high school because it is a laboratory school affiliated with the university, and parents (including a lot of academics) strongly support it. In many small Iowa communities, however, even basic courses such as algebra II and English composition are not provided, for lack of money and staff. Iowa supposedly has the highest overall state standard of education in the country, which is truly frightening considering the basic ignorance that so many of our college students display. The inequality from state to state, and among the schools within each state, is even more outstanding in poor states such as West Virginia.

This constitutional limitation will hinder the United States in developing a volunteer world development, because we may not be able to change the curriculum and the school systems throughout the country. Consequently, everything that I have written in this book may wind up serving as a blueprint for our European and Asian friends. Countries in Europe and Asia do not have our constitutional barriers in changing their educational systems. They have national systems and national standards that produce a consistent product throughout their countries, and that can be rapidly changed by the central government. Thus, in changing curriculum, they do not have to go through all the convolutions that we do. Once they decide that change is in order, it happens. This is one reason why Japan does so much better with its 60 percent "middle" or noncollege-bound students in the vocational area. When MITI (the Ministry of International Trade) determines that certain skills are needed to develop a particular economic sector, then that training is incorporated into high school vocational-training programs, and the student graduates with skills that fit with existing industries. Contrast that with vocational ed classes here, which are primarily baby-sitting facilities where "non–college prep" students diddle around with obsolete automobiles.

Consequently, when Japan decides that an integrated global understanding should be taught to all its students from kindergarten through twelfth grade, that decision will be implemented (and curriculum developed) almost immediately. After all, the Japanese would recognize a market value—beyond volunteer philanthropy—in such a move, because a better global understanding provides skills that are immanently transferable to capturing global markets.

In the United States, there have been some innovative educational ideas proposed by state leaders. In 1989, Governor Thomas Kean of New Jersey favored the direct state control and regulation of inner-city school systems to compensate for their deficiency of local resources. But this is all rather potluck. It may or may not work (a state like New Jersey being noted for incredible corruption). Kean made the proposal just as he was leaving office, so there is some doubt as to whether the new governor will support it. Again we see the nature of our politicians: Go for the media. But on a positive note, there is currently a bill before Congress that would institute a national curriculum, and some believe it may pass within two or three years.

Sadly, deep down, I feel that as a nation we may not ultimately lead this volunteer development process, because our state and local educational processes will not be able to adapt. But that doesn't mean we'll be left out of the picture. I do believe that, on a hit-and-miss basis and combined with the activities of such organizations as the NCRPCV, we can probably impress these global values on at least 15 percent of the school population fairly rapidly. Then, with members of our retired population making their own independent evolution to this kind of work, within a generation (based on a population of 270 million) we could see some 60 million people involved in building our stretch of the pathway to a new world. If 60 million Japanese and 60 million Europeans are behaving the same way, then we will be at least equals in the effort—which maybe is better, anyway. But being unabashedly American, I would naturally like to see us leading in goodness.

But back down to reality: Public television has aired a series called *Learning in America*, which shows the extent of local control and reveals some of the absurdities that occur in the U.S. educational system.[1] One presentation is particularly illuminating because it grapples with the issue of misguided citizen involvement. Specifically, the show takes us to the state of Texas where, through public meetings, local citizens can affect the content taught in their school system. We witness the antics of an older couple who have used their involvement in this process to get content that is "un-American" removed from the history books, and to put content that is supportive of creationism into the science books. Both the political system and the book companies have bowed to their pressure. Basically, two people have been able to introduce what is a rather low-level, isolated curriculum into the entire Texas educational system. And Texas may be the worst case, but unfortunately—if not to the same extreme—a similar debasement of learning is going on throughout the country.

The same PBS presentation gives a totally frightening account of what the textbook companies have been doing lately to sell books. Marketing people—rather than educators—have dominated the editing. The problem with this is summed up by one salesperson who says, "To sell books, the publishers cater to the lowest common denominator." To make a depressing story short, the book companies—under pressure from too many school boards and fundamentalist groups—have simplified and decontroversialized the content of history, cross-culture studies, and civics books so that they will offend no one. As a result, students get a simple, boring presentation that doesn't really educate and certainly doesn't provide the kind of global understanding that our citizens will need in order to function effectively in the next century.

To be fair to the publishers, another reason for simplifying the books is so that inadequately trained teachers can understand and present the material. In the PBS documentary, it is stated that every geography teacher in Texas has the same first name: Coach. Way too many teachers merely follow along with the books as the curriculum guideline, not having the basic skills or content to do anything else. You don't have to be an education specialist to realize that this is just about the lowest and meanest process of education there could be.

In Chapter 1 and again in Chapter 4, some time was spent in presenting Noam Chomsky's political views. Obviously, Chomsky feels that the major barrier to improving education and control of government is government itself. The bigger fear, however, may actually be the school boards, the very local interest groups, and the publishers—who together all too often really control the educational system—for, as mandated by our Constitution, the states themselves have control over how their students shall be educated. Now we know why Hamilton and de Tocqueville expressed their concerns about allowing the local citizenry to control such institutions. A more contemporary patriot—Pogo—has summed it up succinctly: "We have met the enemy, and he is us."

What does the existing educational reality mean for the kind of volunteer world-development system I have been proposing? Well, obviously, it means that many of our young people are not now getting the kind of educational experience necessary to produce a citizenry that understands its place in a global society, nor are they internalizing values that will promote a new world development. It's unfortunate, but that will be the reality for the majority of students for some years to come.

The overall picture is still basically optimistic, however, just because the country is so big. We can probably reach 15 percent of the people within a generation, as proposed in Chapter 7. Some school systems are already developing the necessary curriculum (in the states of California, Iowa, and New York), and are integrating the experience and skills of international organizations such as the NCRPCV. Therefore, there is still hope that, with continued public attention and limited government involvement, the rest of our children will also receive that kind of training. But even assuming that a concerted effort on the part of "education presidents" will continue on into the next century, it could be twenty years before a complete follow-through takes place.

Let's take a closer look at the indications that the process may already be starting. I know of two current efforts to build a global curriculum that are operating from a volunteer-assisted angle. The first is through the oft-mentioned National Council of Returned Peace Corps Volunteers. Utilizing a number of federal grants, several NCRPCV chapters have been developing global education formats and serving as guest lecturers in their communities. Closer to (my) home, the Iowa Peace Institute (IPI) holds global education workshops for elementary and high school teachers and administrators. Consistent with the suggestion made in Chapter 3 that mutually concerned organizations network each other, the IPI is holding a conference to establish a closer linkage with the state chapter of the NCRPCV.

The Iowa project—similar to those of the NCRPCV—focuses on modifying the public school curriculum by regularly bringing into the schools adults who have had international experiences in general. And more specifically, volunteers will show ways by which we can become partners in a world development. There are other states (California and New York) developing similar education projects, and—central to the thesis of this book—the vast majority of such efforts are being handled by volunteers, without the aid of the national government bureaucracies. We can expect these beginnings to expand because all the right elements are in place: a critical mass of experienced people; an improved telecommunications system; and a disenchantment with federal controls, which has made people realize that they have to do it themselves. There is nothing wrong with that.


## ON BEING GOOD GLOBAL CITIZENS—AND HOW WE ARE COMPROMISED

In the advancement toward a global society, we in the United States repeatedly find ourselves compromised by our leaders. In the mid–1980s, the major compromise was the buying of Honduras to serve as base camp for an indirect war with Nicaragua. One consequence of the maneuver was that a number of State Department development projects for Honduras were suddenly open to competitive bidding by consulting groups.

I remember the knee-jerk reaction among the Beltway consulting companies with whom I had worked at one time or another. Several of them got six-month-turnaround Requests for Proposal (RFPs) for water systems and agricultural development programs in Honduras. Nobody was sure whether the infrastructure projects were to be for Honduras, the Contras, or our visiting troops; but there were millions available, and the development companies were jumping over each other to get some of it. My company didn't get the grant, so it's easy for me to say that I wouldn't have prostituted myself by working for such a blatant payoff. The main point here is that this kind of economic development effort isn't really all that constructive because the recipients know where it comes from and why, and when it will end. And certainly, every time this kind of U.S. maneuver is exposed here, it gives our children all the more reason to be cynical about our political objectives in the world.

If we are really serious about creating a new world, this is not the way to go about it. At some point, we are going to have to elect a majority of decent, honest politicians who can pick the political system up out of the gutter and work for a long-term, stable global order. You're saying fat chance, and you're probably right. However, that inability to get honest leaders is what makes the volunteer pathway to a world development all the more necessary. When President Bush talks about his 1,000 points of light, what he may be subconsciously telling us is that the political process is inherently corrupt. Consequently, it is up to the average citizen to devise new institutions that will change the world. Maybe the current presidency will serve a useful purpose, then, in promoting and confirming the simple message that people can transcend government through volunteerism and be responsible for reforming their own political system and creating a new world order.

## AN EXPERIMENT IN VOLUNTEER DEVELOPMENT

Halfway through writing this book, I began a development effort in Baja California to experiment on integrating volunteer inputs into a major development effort. The central thesis was that microinvestment plus volunteer input can produce macro-development in a given country. The physical site was a Mexican *ejido* (one of the jointly owned landholdings that were granted to subsistence farmers from the expropriation of private land-holdings after the Mexican Revolution of 1910). This particular ejido has fifteen miles of sandy beaches within a total holding of 40,000 acres. The concern of the *ejiditarios* was to develop the property without giving control to the *gringos*. Since I was working in the area on a commercial shrimp production system, they came to me for advice.

The first ideas were pretty much hopeless. They had figured on building three-bedroom cottages that would rent for US $1,000 per month and cost $50,000 to build. This was based on an assumption that the cabins would be occupied for the full year. After I was able to convince them that most beach hotels anticipate only a half-year season of full occupancy, and after taking the going rate of interest into consideration, we calculated about a $5,000 loss per year for each cottage under the best of circumstances.

We began talking about the strengths of the ejido—one of which is a skill in building with adobe. After some discussion, it was established that everybody did indeed already know how to work with the material. Even more importantly, I was able to show them that they could build a cabin of adobe for about $1,000. After only six months' occupancy, they would have their investment back.

So where does the volunteer network come into the picture? Well, after the preliminary discussions were over and I had become a socio (a member of the ejido), I made a few phone calls and got some money together. Then I called up a volunteer engineer whose expertise is water systems to work on improving the spring water-source. Another engineer who works on septic systems contributed the design for a water conserving system; another designed a solar hot-water unit. And several volunteers with carpentry skills will be spending their weekends in Baja, laying out foundations and teaching basic carpentry skills. Of course, these people get something besides the healthful benefits that volunteerism provides. They'll also be enjoying fifteen miles of private beach and surf and fishing in a unique environment that looks like eighteenth-century California. But there is nothing wrong with that. There's no law that says you have to wear a hair shirt while helping others.

The important outcome, however, is that the ejiditarios are receiving several thousand dollars worth of engineering advice free and have a no-interest, up-front loan that won't have to be repaid until the beach cabins show a profit (at which time the principal and investment will be repaid on a fifty-fifty split basis). Thus, the people will be able to develop their new village industry basically risk free. And at the same time, we are going to be able to protect and preserve this unique environment so that people living in the twenty-first century will be able to see what eighteenth-century California looked like. In a case like this, everybody wins. And the project was accomplished in less time than it takes just to get a proposal started through the traditional bureaucratic funding process.

This is just one example of how one can operationalize development efforts on a volunteer basis, as has been proposed throughout this book. The key—as illustrated by the cooperation of assorted engineers in this project—is that there already exists a network of volunteers who have the appropriate skills and a global viewpoint. They can be called into action whenever and wherever a development situation requires their help. In the Baja California project, the network existed through my contacts, but the reason it came together was that the people who volunteered their services had internalized a world view that such international work is worthwhile and important to them. They will be available again, as future projects need them. And it has been the position of this book throughout that we can organize these networks on a macro scale as well, for development efforts throughout the world. In fact, given the ease with which I was able to enlist the aid of volunteers in this project, it is even possible that I have been underestimating the willingness of people to become involved in a world-development effort.

## REFLECTIONS

In that now continuous economic war between the Americans and the Asians, it has been said that the Americans will lose because they are too sentimental and not cutthroat enough in their economic behavior. It has also been said that Americans would waste time crying about helping others less fortunate than themselves—something that, it has been said, Asians by nature would not. A friend of mine tells me that in the cooperative lunch program at his institute, the Chinese scientists race to the front of the line and pick out all the meat before anybody else can get to the food—something he feels that Americans would never do. On a larger scale, the Chinese government has (more than once) shown its basic ruthlessness through its willingness to sacrifice an entire generation of students to preserve power, as it did in Tiananmen Square in June 1989.

Ask the Seven Civilized Nations (the Native American Indian tribes) or the imprisoned Japanese-American citizens during World War II about the basic sentimentality and fairness of Americans, and you'll get a different opinion. But in its neurotic,

convoluted, distorted, and Christian-biased way, there is something to that mythical image of us. And if that underlying concern about fairness in helping the less fortunate will stimulate
the acculturation of a global concern in our children, then we
as a country will be none the worse for it.

## THE WORLD TAX

In my 1987 book *Organizational Change and the Third World*, I
proposed that one way to finance Third World development
might be through a world tax of the rich countries. This could
be a powerhouse of funding: Considering that there is roughly
$4 trillion of GNP in the twelve primary developed countries,
even a 0.1 percent tax would produce $4 billion for development.

In that book, I left it somewhat ambiguous as to who should
monitor and disburse the funds and projects. Let me now make
it unambiguous. The people in charge of all this development
money would be volunteers—not bureaucrats. All of the politics
need to be removed from this arena. Development money can
no longer be used to purchase governments—as, for instance,
the United States is wont to do in Central America. We should
all know by now that "rice Christians" accept no real internalization of their "benefactor's" values.

I believe that a world tax could indeed be legislated within
each of the developed countries, as volunteer efforts expand and
as we produce a more sustained global concern in our citizenry.
Even in the United States, politicians do listen if people scream
in their ear long enough. Only about 40 percent of the eligible
population votes in this country. Ultimately, that 40 percent
could be composed of those people who have internalized a
global-development value system and would probably vote for
such a tax. In Europe, with its 90 percent who vote, one would
expect even smoother sailing.

And in fact, there has already been some international pressure to implement this idea. In February 1989 more than 140
scientists met in New Delhi at a conference on global warming.
"A major recommendation by the delegates at the three day
meeting was a tax on gasoline and other fossil fuels in Western
nations." Their feeling was that "such taxes could assist re-

forestation programs in poor countries and help finance alternatives to industries that produce chlorofluorocarbons."[2]

Fortunately—to reduce the hypocrisy index—the delegates also suggested that developing countries get their act together on such environmentally degrading practices as deforestation and uncontrolled population increase. This will be absolutely necessary if the Third World really expects the developed world to tax itself. In any case, the recommendation is a start. Its only major problem is that it would rely on international and state bureaucracies to disperse the funds, instead of volunteer organizations.

## THE PATHWAY TO A NEW WORLD

We as individual citizens operating in development groups and organizations will largely have to create the pathway to a new world on our own. Governments have shown that they reflect the peculiar neuroses and psychoses of those who have been elected or otherwise acceded to power.

To make that change ourselves, we need a newly educated citizenry that understands its place in global society and will do its duty in helping others. The means at our disposal—with or without central government help—have already been outlined in earlier chapters.

And should such an active and aware citizenry come to pass, then—in the end—we will be living in societies whose governments are simply adjuncts to the continual process of people working directly with other people to solve their economic problems. In a truly participatory democracy, there is no need to go through a politician to get the job done. One may need a facilitator who knows how to gather resources. But the facilitator stays out of the process itself, because she or he knows too that the inherent corruptibility of the political process will stand in the way of success. Such facilitators are perhaps best described by Lao-tzu, who said that he who leads best is he who—when the group discusses its accomplishments—can say, "We did it ourselves."

Under the present electoral system, of course, there is only the slimmest of chances that our leaders would meet such a qualification. But times are changing. As Eastern bloc citizens press for democratic reforms, it is very possible that we as a nation will come to expect more from our own system of government and will develop an electoral process capable of producing politicians whose hearts are pure, whose operational styles are facilitative, and whose potential for corruption can be controlled by volunteer watch committees.

In the meantime—to the end of creating a new world that will be of the people instead of only for the people, and that will serve all people—the cynicism brought on by the atrocious behavior of too many of our leaders does serve a useful purpose. Via the telecommunications breakthroughs described mostly in Chapter 6, the average fed-up person can really do something that affects our political evolution. Average citizens can in fact build the pathway to a new world—with the aid of governments that support, facilitate, and do not dominate the process. All the necessary elements are there. With a little bit of luck, we can make it.

## NOTES

1. *Learning in America*, PBS Television, April 20, 1989.
2. San Bernardino *Sun*, March 5, 1989.

# Selected Bibliography

Arndt, C., and Everett, S. *Education for a World Society: 11th Yearbook of the John Dewey Society*. New York: Harper and Brooks, 1951.

Bennis, Warren. *Changing Organizations*. New York: Doubleday, 1988.

Bleakley, K. Address to the Ninth Annual Third World Conference, Omaha, Nebraska, October 1988.

Bok, Cicela. *A Conversation with Bill Moyers*. PBS Television, October 6, 1988.

Brazelton, Barry. *A Conversation with Bill Moyers*. PBS Television, October 2, 1988.

Campbell, Joseph. *The Masks of God: Creative Mythology*. New York: Viking, 1968.

————. *The Power of Myth*. New York: Doubleday, 1988.

Cassell, Frank. "The Corporation and Community Realities and Myths." In *Fundamentals of Management: Selected Readings*, ed. James Donnelly, Jr. Dallas: Business Publications, 1975, pp. 35–80.

Chomsky, Noam. *A Conversation with Bill Moyers*. PBS Television. September 20, 1988.

Derkousky, Oleg. Address to the Ninth Annual Third World Conference, Omaha, Nebraska, October 1988.

Des Moines *Register*, Agribusiness section, January 15, 1989.

Drucker, Peter. *The Frontiers of Management*. New York: Truman Talley Books, 1986.

Feigenbaum, E., and McCorduck, P. *The Fifth Generation*. New York: Addison-Wesley, 1983.

Growald, E., and Luks, A. "The Healing Power of . . ." *American Health* (March 1988).

Jedlicka, A. *Organizational Change and the Third World: Designs for the Twenty-first Century*. New York: Praeger, 1987.

———. *Organization for Rural Development*. New York: Praeger, 1977.

Leakey, Richard. *People of the Lake: Mankind and Its Beginning*. New York: Anchor/Doubleday, 1978.

Likert, Rensis. "The Nature of Highly Effective Groups." In *Readings on Behavior in Organizations*, ed. Edgar Huse; James Bowditch; and Dalmar Fisher. New York: Addison-Wesley, 1975.

McGregor, D. *The Human Side of Enterprise*. New York: McGraw-Hill, 1960.

Miller, A. "The New Volunteerism." *Newsweek*, February 8, 1988.

*National Council of Returned Peace Corps Volunteers Newsletter*, December 1988, pp. 2–3.

Norland, R.; J. Contreras; and D. Newell. "The Other Aid Network." *Newsweek*, July 27, 1987.

*Poughkeepsie Journal*, January 1, 1989, p. 1B.

Skinner, B. F. *Beyond Freedom and Dignity*. New York: Alfred A. Knopf, 1974.

Wolin, Sheldon. *A Conversation with Bill Moyers*. PBS Television, December 28, 1988.

# Index

## ABOUT THE AUTHOR

ALLEN JEDLICKA is a Professor of International Business and Organizational Behavior and the Coordinator of International Business Programs at the University of Northern Iowa. He has spent twenty years researching organizational change in Third World countries and is the author of *Organization for Rural Development* (Praeger, 1977) and *Organizational Change and the Third World* (Praeger, 1987). Dr. Jedlicka holds a B.A. from San Diego State College and a Ph.D. from Northwestern University.